WETHERSFIELD INSTITUTE

Proceedings, 1991

THE MIND AND HEART
OF THE CHURCH

The Mind
and Heart
of the Church

Papers Presented at a Conference
Sponsored by the Wethersfield Institute
New York City, September 20, 1991

EDITED, WITH A PREFACE BY
RALPH MCINERNY

IGNATIUS PRESS   SAN FRANCISCO

Cover by Riz Boncan Marsella

"Christ Calling St. Peter", historiated initial "S" illuminated by
Pelligrino di Mariano, from an Antiphonary, Italy, Siena, Ca.
1471, The Bernard H. Breslauer Collection, New York. This leaf
is included in the exhibition of the Breslauer Collection, of illu-
mination presented at the Pierpont Morgan Library, New York,
and is discussed and illustrated, with the entire collection, in the
accompanying catalogue, "The Bernard H. Breslauer Collection
of Manuscript Illuminations." Special thanks to Mr. Breslauer
for the use of his manuscript.

WETHERSFIELD INSTITUTE
STATEMENT OF PURPOSE

The purpose of Wethersfield Institute is to promote a clear understanding of Catholic teaching and practice, and to explore the cultural and intellectual dimensions of the Catholic Faith. The Institute does so in practical ways that include seminars, colloquies and conferences especially as they pursue our goals on a scientific and scholarly level. The Institute publishes its proceedings.

It is also interested in projects that advance those subjects. The Institute usually sponsors them directly, but also joins with accredited agencies that share our interests.

CONTENTS

CONTRIBUTORS

KENNETH BAKER, S.J., is the Editor-in-Chief of *Homiletic and Pastoral Review* and president of the board of directors of the Fellowship of Catholic Scholars.

JUDE P. DOUGHERTY is Dean of the School of Philosophy at the Catholic University of America and editor of the *Review of Metaphysics*.

ROBERT A. GEORGE teaches philosophy of law and civil liberties at Princeton University. He served on the staff of Chief Justice of the Supreme Court William Rehnquist during the 1989–90 term.

JAMES HITCHCOCK is Professor of History at St. Louis University. He is the author of several books, including *The Pope and the Jesuits* and *Years of Crisis*.

RONALD P. MCARTHUR is the founding President of Thomas Aquinas College. After twenty years in that post, he now devotes his retirement to lecturing and to philosophy. He is this year's recipient of the Wethersfield Award.

PAUL V. MANKOWSKI, S.J., is a Harvard University Ph.D. candidate in the Department of Near Eastern Languages. He has been active in Operation Rescue, having twice been jailed.

DR. JANET E. SMITH is in the Philosophy Department at the University of Dallas. Her long-awaited book, *Humanae Vitae: A Generation Later* has just been published by Catholic University of America Press.

DR. ALICE VON HILDEBRAND was Professor of Philosophy at Hunter College until her retirement. She is now devoting her time to writing and lecturing.

RALPH McINERNY

PREFACE

While the theme of the 1991 Wethersfield Conference, The Mind and Heart of the Church, might seem uncharacteristically broad or ill focused, the perceptive reader of the papers gathered together in this volume will find them far from disparate. Indeed, as our theme suggests, there are two major threads running through the following essays.

The first concerns the situation in Catholic institutions of higher learning, our colleges and universities. We had thought of devoting the conference entirely to the recent Apostolic Constitution on Catholic Universities, *Ex corde ecclesiae*. To do so, however, would have precluded contributions having to do with the Church as lived in the lives of all of us, academic or not. Rather than choose and thereby exclude, it occurred to us that papers could be commissioned that would complement one another, some addressing the mind of the Church, others her heart.

Father Kenneth Baker's paper bears directly on the Apostolic Constitution on Catholic Universities and provides a crisp account and analysis of its contents. Professor James Hitchcock, with the exuberance and panache of the tenured academic, gave us a historian's perception of how we have gotten from where we were to where we now are. Professor Robert George gave a precise and analytical introduction to the vexed question of academic freedom. Dean Jude Dougherty, with the authority of decades as the head of the prestigious School of Philosophy at the Catholic University of America, conveyed the principled outlook that has been a major factor in keeping the School of

Philosophy on an even keel. Dr. Ronald McArthur, founder and first President of Thomas Aquinas College, spoke out of his experience as tutor in one of the brightest spots in American Catholic higher education. McArthur is also the recipient of the 1991 Wethersfield Award for Excellence.

Father Paul Mankowski turned the attention of the audience to the Church's worship and in his characteristically incisive and witty way spoke of the liturgy, as it ought to be and as it is degraded by liturgical ad libbers. Women's libbers of the kind that dominates the secular world have no place in the Church, and Janet E. Smith, having made that point, celebrated the wisdom of the Church's teaching on woman. Finally, a perennial favorite of our September conference, Alice Von Hildebrand, reflected on the mystery of suffering, with special reference to women.

The auditorium of the Donnell Library was again filled with an enthusiastic audience for the Wethersfield Conference. The program did not permit extended discussion, but the evening banquet more than made up for that, providing an extended opportunity for formal and informal questioning of the speakers. Dr. McArthur's remarks on receiving the Wethersfield Award were profoundly moving.

On behalf of E. Lisk Wyckhoff, President of the Homeland Foundation, and Monsignor Eugene V. Clark, President of the Wethersfield Institute, I am delighted to present these papers to a wider audience.

PRESENTATION OF
THE WETHERSFIELD AWARD
SEPTEMBER 20, 1991

The 1991 Wethersfield Award for Excellence has been presented to Ronald McArthur, one of the most famous graduates of the *Faculté de Philosophie* of Laval University, a worthy protégé of its dean, Charles DeKoninck, and an exponent of the letter and spirit of the teaching of St. Thomas Aquinas. How fitting, if not inevitable, that Ronald McArthur should have been the founder and first President of Thomas Aquinas College, Santa Paula, California. There, McArthur and his colleagues have devoted themselves to teaching, eschewing the siren song of *soi-disant* research for the living communal and personal quest for truth. In *A Man for All Seasons*, Robert Bolt shows us Thomas More advising the ambitious Richard Rich to leave the temptations of the court and devote himself to teaching. Rich wonders who then would ever hear of him, who would even know if he did well. St. Thomas More replies: "You will know, your students will know, and God will know." After long years of uphill effort, Ronald McArthur knows what he and his friends have accomplished. Needless to say, God knows too. As for their students, it is through them that many have learned of the great work going on at Thomas Aquinas College. A significant number of its graduates have entered the priesthood or religious life. Others have fanned out over the nation, into teaching, into law, into government, into publishing, into a variety of forms of lay participation in the work of the Church. Most have married and begun families that will assure Thomas Aquinas College an inexhaustible supply of future students. The Wethersfield Institute—whose founder, Chauncey Stillman, held Thomas Aquinas College in high regard—is delighted to acknowledge the contribution to Catholic higher education, and to the Church, of Ronald P. McArthur.

KENNETH BAKER, S.J.

POPE JOHN PAUL II AND
THE CATHOLIC UNIVERSITY

Pope John Paul II is a man of enormous talent and energy. In his thirteen years as Supreme Pontiff he has, in effect, rewritten the book on how to be Pope. In his more than fifty trips abroad, he has brought the Good News of salvation to men and women on all levels of society. My topic today is "Pope John Paul II and the Catholic University". It is not a difficult topic, since the Pope has spoken to university groups of professors and students on many occasions, both in Rome and on his pastoral visits in most parts of the world. He has stated clearly on several occasions what he thinks about the Catholic university.

The Pope sees the Church, depository of the truth about the world, about man, and about God, as the source or origin of the Catholic university. The opening words of the recent (1990) Apostolic Constitution on Catholic Universities, written by the Pope, declare that the Catholic university is "born from the heart of the church".[1] Central to his thinking about the university is that it is a place where the members are united by a common search for truth and a desire to communicate the known truth to others.

Early in his pontificate the new Pope spoke again and again about the importance of *truth*; he often puts it in the combination "the truth about nature, about man, and about God". The word *truth* is a key word in his vocabulary. He understands it in the scholastic sense of "the conformity of the mind to the thing" as logical truth, and the conformity of the thing to the mind of God as ontological truth. For him, truth is objective, knowable by the human mind and communicable to others.

In the Pope's mind the search for truth and the communication of the truth constitute the raison d'être of a Catholic university. He does not hesitate to say that the Church possesses truth about the world, man, and God; that the truth can be communicated to others; and that it must be expanded by further research in an atmosphere of freedom at the Catholic university.

It is a truism of philosophy that all men naturally desire to know. In his talk to the faculty at the Catholic University of America on October 7, 1979, the Pope said that the deepest and noblest aspiration of the human person is "the desire to come to the knowledge of the truth". He also said that the Catholic university is committed to "the service of truth and charity".[2] In *Ex corde ecclesiae*, the Pope wrote: "It is the honor and responsibility of a Catholic university to consecrate itself without reserve to the cause of truth. . . . A Catholic university is distinguished by its free search for the whole truth about nature, man and God."[3] That is vintage John Paul II.

For centuries it has been customary in Church documents about education to stress the right of the Church to conduct schools of all kinds. This right flows from the command of Jesus to the apostles to go into the whole world and teach the Good News of salvation (see Mt 28:18–20). So the Church of Christ is a teaching Church. Teaching can be done in many ways— from the pulpit, by catechetical instruction, in books and pamphlets, but especially in schools. From the earliest times the Church established schools: "From these schools arose the universities, those glorious institutions of the Middle Ages which, from their beginning, had the Church as their most bountiful mother and patroness."[4]

To the CUA faculty the Pope said, "The relationship to truth explains, therefore, the historical bond between the university and the Church. Because she herself finds her origin and her growth in the words of Christ, which are the liberating truth (cf. Jn 8:32), the Church has always tried to stand by the institutions that serve, and cannot but serve, the knowledge of truth. The Church can rightfully boast of being in a sense the mother of universities."[5]

Because of the deposit of the Faith, the Catholic university has an immense treasure of divine and revealed truth to be studied and to be communicated to students. It is a place where both the natural and the supernatural can be investigated in complete freedom; they are not totally separated from each other, nor are they confused; they are related to each other according to a sort of hierarchy of truths.

The Catholic university is not imprisoned in the world of nature alone; it is open to the supernatural, to God, to divine truth, and so to the totality of all truth. This is a key point in John Paul II's understanding of the nature of a truly Catholic university. There is no real opposition between natural science and revealed truth; there cannot be, since all reality, and hence all truth, flows from the one God who created everything. The Pope says that it is the special task of the Catholic university "to unite existentially by intellectual effort two orders of reality that too frequently tend to be placed in opposition as though they were antithetical: the search for truth and the certainty of already knowing the fount of truth".[6]

Through her Catholic universities the Church, "expert in humanity . . . explores the mysteries of humanity and of the world, clarifying them in the light of revelation".[7] We are witness to tremendous advances in science and technology —developments that have dramatically changed the world in which we live. The wealth and variety of new knowledge necessarily raise the question in the minds of many about the meaning of it all. The Pope sees the ultimate meaning of all this diversity in Jesus Christ and his Gospel. "If it is the responsibility of every university to search for such meaning, a Catholic university is called in a particular way to respond to this need: Its Christian inspiration enables it to include the moral, spiritual and religious dimension in its research and to evaluate the attainments of science and technology in the perspective of the totality of the human person."[8]

In a Catholic university there is an essential connection between its Catholic commitment and what it does as a university. In 1979 the Pope said to a group of educators in the United States, "Catholic education is above all a question of communicating Christ, of helping to form Christ in the lives of others." And again, "The cause of Catholic education is the cause of Jesus Christ and of His Gospel at the service of man."[9]

What is a Catholic university in the mind of John Paul II? On several occasions he has listed what he considers to be the three characteristics of a Catholic university.[10]

First, the Catholic university must make a positive contribution to the Church and to society through a high level of scientific research. There is always the drive to find the truth. But it must find "its ultimate and deep meaning in Christ, in His message of salvation which embraces man in his totality, and in the teaching of the Church. All this presupposes the promotion of an integral culture, that is, one that aims at the complete development of the human person; one in which emphasis is laid on the values of intelligence, will, conscience, and brotherhood, all of which are based on God the Creator and have been marvelously exalted in Christ (cf. *Gaudium et spes*, n. 61)."[11]

Second, the Catholic university "must form men who are really outstanding for their knowledge, ready to exercise important functions in society and to bear witness to their faith before the world".[12] The Catholic university strives to promote in both professors and students "a more and more harmonious synthesis between faith and reason, between faith and culture, between faith and life".[13]

Third, the Catholic university "must be an environment in which Christianity is alive and operating. It is an essential vocation of the Catholic university to bear witness that it is a community seriously and sincerely engaged in scientific research, but also visibly characterized by a real Christian life."[14] The Pope also has a word for professors: they are not merely transmitters of knowledge; they must also be witnesses to true Christian life in their work and in their dealings with others.

In summary, then, the Catholic university is a place where creative research takes place under the light and inspiration of the Gospel of Jesus Christ. It is a place where Christian professors communicate knowledge to students, where they form them with a harmonious synthesis of faith and reason. It is a place where professors and students form a true Christian community of scholars, where they create a real university family engaged in the pursuit of truth and goodness.[15]

The purpose of the Church is to save all mankind by preaching Christ to them and bringing about their conversion. So she strives to bring the Good News to every dimension of human existence, including that of the intellect. Wherever men are, that is where the Church strives to be. Culture is a complexity of customs, language, thought patterns, and attitudes that characterize various groups of human beings. The Pope says that "the Church carries out her mission of evangelizing also by advancing human culture".[16]

The notion of "culture" recurs frequently in the thinking of the Pope when he speaks of the Catholic university. He sees the university as an essential arm of the evangelizing mission of the Church. It is an apostolate of the mind that extends into every dimension of human culture. In the thinking of the Pope, without the light of the Gospel, human culture is incomplete; it is partial; it is defective. Human culture needs the message of the Gospel:

> Through the encounter which it establishes between the unfathomable richness of the salvific message of the Gospel and the variety and immensity of the fields of knowledge in which that richness is incarnated by it, a Catholic university enables the church to institute an incomparably fertile dialogue with people of every culture. Man's life is given dignity by culture, and while he finds his fullness in Christ, there can be no doubt that the

Gospel, which reaches and renews him in every dimension, is also fruitful for the culture in which he lives.[17]

When speaking about the relationship between the Gospel and culture, the Pope often uses the word *permeate* or a synonym. In the foreword of his Apostolic Constitution *Ex corde ecclesiae* he wrote: "The very power of the Gospel should permeate thought patterns, standards of judgment, and norms of behavior; in a word, it is necessary that the whole of human culture be steeped in the Gospel" (no. 1). Thus, when a culture is influenced by the Gospel, it is an aid to evangelization: "A division between faith and culture is more than a small impediment to evangelization, while a culture penetrated with the Christian spirit is an instrument that favors the spreading of the Good News."[18]

Because of its Christian inspiration the Catholic university can include the moral, spiritual, and religious dimensions in its research and teaching and can evaluate the results and claims of modern science in light of "the totality of the human person".[19] It is free therefore to include the transcendent dimension of the human person, something that is a priori excluded in the secular and materialistic approach to man and the world at public and state universities.

In this regard, John Paul II makes an unusual and, to the secular mind, absurd claim that commitment to Catholicism makes one impartial in the search for truth. For he says in *Ex corde ecclesiae*, "By its Catholic character a university is made more capable of conducting an impartial search for truth, a search that is neither subordinated to nor conditioned by particular interests of any kind."[20] In other words, the Catholic university is not captive to any ideology or any "ism". It is truly universal and therefore not partisan because, in submission to the Lord, it knows the truth that sets one free (see Jn 8:32).

It is clear that the Pope thinks the university is a very important factor in the shaping of culture. For most of his adult life he has been associated with a university in one way or another. Even as Archbishop of Krakow he had regular contact with university students. He has shown many times on his trips abroad that he loves to meet with students. He said that these meetings give him "a well-founded hope for a new flowering of Christian culture in the rich and varied context of our changing times".[21] On another occasion he wrote that a Catholic university is "a primary and privileged place for a fruitful dialogue between the Gospel and culture".[22]

In the introduction of *Ex corde ecclesiae*, the Pope said, "Finally, I turn to the whole church, convinced that Catholic universities are essential to her growth and to the development of Christian culture and human progress. For this reason, the entire ecclesial community is invited to give its support to Catholic institutions of higher education and to assist them in their process of development and renewal" (no. 11). The Pope is deeply convinced that a Catholic university is "one of the best instruments that the church offers to our age, which is searching for certainty and wisdom".[23]

Ever since the publication of *Evangelii nuntiandi* by Pope Paul VI in 1975, the Popes have repeatedly reminded Catholics of the need for Catholic evangelization. In this context, John Paul II sees the Catholic university as a powerful instrument of evangelization. He says that the students of these universities should "witness the faith to the world".[24] Again, "By its very nature, each Catholic university makes an important contribution to the Church's work of evangelization."[25] The same idea pops up frequently when the Pope talks about the purpose of the Catholic university. He sees no opposition between scientific research and spreading the Gospel: "Scientific study and evangelization go together; the one supports and sustains the other."[26]

In order to be truthfully designated "Catholic", a university must have a living, essential relationship to the hierarchy. If it is not under the hierarchy in some way, it is simply not Catholic, no matter what name it might give itself. Early in his pontificate, in 1979, to the faculty at the Catholic University of America, the Pope said, "If then your universities and colleges are institutionally committed to the Christian message and if they are part of the Catholic community of evangelization, it follows that they have an essential relationship to the hierarchy of the Church" (no. 6).

The Pope insists that the Catholic university is a part of the body of the Church. As such it has a special bond with the local bishop and with the Holy See "by reason of the service to unity which it is called to render to the whole church".[27] A result of this is submission to the Magisterium of the Church. Here is how the Pope puts it: "One consequence of its essential relationship to the church is that the institutional fidelity of the university to the Christian message includes a recognition of and adherence to the teaching authority of the church in matters of faith and morals. Catholic members of the university community are also called to a personal fidelity to the church with all that this implies."[28]

Since the local bishop has a special responsibility for the teaching of the Faith and the administration of the sacraments, he has a special responsibility to help promote the Catholic identity of the Catholic university. But even when bishops are not involved directly in the governance of a university, they "should be seen not as external agents but as participants in the life of the Catholic university".[29]

When it comes to theological research and teaching, the Pope insists that the university must, if it is to be Catholic, be guided by Scripture, Tradition, and the Magisterium of the Church. Thus, he said to the council of the International Federation of Catholic Universities in February 1979, "As for theological research properly speaking, by definition it cannot exist without seeking its source and its regulation in Scripture and Tradition, in the experience and decisions of the church handed down by the magisterium throughout the course of the centuries" (no. 3).

In October of that year the Pope said the same thing to the

faculty at the Catholic University of America: "But true theological scholarship, and by the same token, theological teaching, cannot exist and be fruitful without seeking its inspiration and its source in the Word of God as contained in Sacred Scripture and in the Sacred Tradition of the Church as interpreted by the authentic magisterium throughout history (cf. *Dei verbum* 10)" (no. 6).

This means, of course, that Catholic theology can be developed and taught only within the prescribed limits of Scripture, Tradition, and the Magisterium. Thus, one cannot declare oneself independent of the Magisterium and still claim to be "Catholic" as that word is understood by the Church and the Pope.

In summary, John Paul II defined the nature of the Catholic university when he wrote: "Every Catholic university, as a university, is an academic community which, in a rigorous and critical fashion, assists in the protection and advancement of human dignity and of a cultural heritage through research, teaching and various services offered to the local, national and international communities."[30] He goes on to say that the university enjoys "institutional autonomy" and guarantees its members *academic freedom* "so long as the rights of the individual person and of the community are preserved within the confines of the truth and the common good".[31]

The Pope's understanding of "academic freedom" is very different from that which is current in American universities. For him it is a limited freedom, just as all freedoms are limited, because man is a limited creature. According to the Pope, academic freedom is limited by the rights of individual persons, by the rights of the community, and by the just claims of truth and the common good. Here we come again to his understanding of truth as a reality that is objective, attainable, and capable of being known with certainty. So the Pope's understanding of the nature of truth, as was noted at the beginning, is very different from the sceptical and relativistic approach that is dominant in Western secular thinking.

I would like to conclude this presentation by offering a thumbnail sketch of John Paul II's understanding of the Catholic university. The key idea is the truth about nature, man, and God. Because the Church has been commanded by Christ to proclaim the whole truth, she has the right and duty to establish universities. They have three basic functions: (1) to conduct research, (2) to teach and form students in the truth, and (3) to form a community of Christian scholars who strive to advance human culture by bearing witness to the Gospel and by scientific research that embraces the totality of the human person.

The members of a Catholic community of scholars should bear witness to their Faith in all their endeavors. The university itself, as part of the Church with an essential relationship to the hierarchy, is an important instrument of evangelization. One of the goals of the Catholic university is to permeate human culture with the spirit of the Gospel. One of the ways in which it does this is by dialogue with individuals and cultures. When culture is permeated with the Gospel it becomes integral because it embraces all dimensions of the human person.

NOTES

[1] *Ex corde ecclesiae*, no. 1. The English text is presented in *Origins*, Oct. 4, 1990, vol. 20, no. 17, pp. 265–76. It will be cited here as ECE.

[2] John Paul II to the faculty at the Catholic University of America (CUA), Oct. 7, 1979. The talk is printed in Daughters of St. Paul, *The Messages of Justice and Peace* (Boston: 1979), p. 254, no. 1.

[3] ECE, no. 4.

[4] *Sapientia christiana*. Apostolic Constitution of John Paul II, 1979. See *L'Osservatore Romano*, English ed., June 4, 1979, p. 3, foreword II.

[5] John Paul II to the faculty at CUA, no. 4.

[6] ECE, no. 1.

[7] Ibid., no. 3.

[8] Ibid., no. 7.

[9] Message to the National Catholic Education Association, Apr. 1979, in *To the Church in America* (Boston: St. Paul Editions, 1981), pp. 49–50.

[10] *Messages of John Paul II*, vol. 2 (Boston: St. Paul Editions, 1979), pp. 332–33: address to students at Catholic universities in Mexico at Guadalupe (cited henceforth as Guadalupe). Address on Feb. 24, 1979, to the Council of the International Federation of Catholic Universities in *Messages*, vol. 2, p. 442. The three characteristics are also listed briefly in ECE, no. 1.

[11] Guadalupe, p. 332, no. 2.

[12] Ibid.

[13] Ibid.

[14] Ibid.

[15] Ibid.

[16] *Sapientia christiana*, foreword I.

[17] ECE, no. 6.

[18] *Sapientia christiana*, foreword I.

[19] ECE, no. 7.

[20] Ibid.

[21] ECE, no. 2.

[22] *Sapientia christiana*, no. 43.

[23] ECE, no. 10.

[24] Ibid.

[25] ECE, no. 49.

[26] Address to the faculty of the Gregorian University, Rome, 1979, in "John Paul II at the Gregorian University and the Biblical Institute", a pamphlet printed by the Gregorian University Press (1980), p. 22, no. 6.

[27] ECE, no. 27.

[28] Ibid.
[29] ECE, no. 28.
[30] Ibid.
[31] ECE, no. 12.

JAMES HITCHCOCK

LEARNING AMONG THE RUINS

Even more than the Church, the university encapsulates the
entire modern cultural crisis, because the university defines itself as the bearer of the totality of culture, past and present.

The phenomenon loosely called "the sixties" remains the
crucial episode in university, church, and society at large. What
happened in the period roughly from 1965 to 1975 was the
greatest challenge that higher education in the United States
has ever faced, and there is no way of concealing the fact that,
for all their vaunted "openness" and the great stores of wisdom
they supposedly guarded, the universities failed in that crisis
in ways that have brought on a slow spiritual death.

The obvious death wound of the universities was their inabil-
ity to resist, or even to express principled disagreement with,
naked acts of coercion and terrorism intended to prevent them
from carrying out their activities. Classes were forcibly can-
celed by threatening students; curricula and rules concerning
student behavior were precipitously "reformed" under similar
kinds of threats; vandalism to buildings and occasional violence
against persons occurred. If the university, as its devotees had
been fond of boasting, was the one place where the rule of
reason was supreme, that monarch proved wholly ineffective
when confronted with determined acts of revolution, the re-
jection of all reasoned discourse.

Mere cowardice on the part of faculty and administrators
explains some of this, but not all. Anyone who lived through
the campus crisis of two decades ago recalls how the paral-
ysis of those ostensibly in charge of the institution—faculty,

administrators, often trustees as well—was induced at least as much by a troubled uncertainty. Many of the priests of reason simply could not bring themselves to state unequivocally that the assaults directed at them violated their own sacred principles. In the student rebels they saw something of themselves, and part of their being, if it did not actually sympathize, was nonetheless prepared to "understand" quite liberally.

One of the great frustrations engendered by the New Left was the fact that some of its criticisms of higher education were justified. But even these were advanced only semicoherently and simplistically, intermingled with a great deal of pernicious nonsense. Thus a possible opportunity to reform the universities authentically instead produced changes that were almost all destructive.

The validity of the New Left's criticism was in its charge that modern higher education has allowed itself to become merely pragmatic and instrumental and has lost sight of any possible transcendent purpose. The reasons for this are primarily institutional, not personal, as illustrated in the fact that in the modern university a devout religious believer may sincerely see no way in which his faith should inform his teaching or research and may even think that such influence would be subversive of the nature of education. Indeed, as education has come to be defined, it would be.

The professionalization of higher education has produced unfortunate results that are too familiar even to need enumeration —faculty often interested in narrow research projects with only slight relevance to a real education, students permitted (in some cases forced) into programs involving similar kinds of narrow specialization, the "smorgasbord" approach to education that breeds superficiality and eclecticism.

Such effects are inevitable under the terms of modern disciplinary specialization because no discipline can claim the right to evaluate any other discipline, and thus no discipline can even define its own place in the hierarchy of knowledge. There is simply no theoretical way, within the established disciplinary perspective, in which a university can declare that some courses are more important than others or that certain courses constitute an irreducible core of genuine liberal education. Thus, as often noted, the modern curriculum is in practice almost entirely the result of academic politics—particular disciplines tend to gain larger pieces of the curriculum for themselves mainly on the basis of the political skills of their practitioners. Any claim of disciplinary importance is met with the counterclaim that the claimant is merely defending an unfairly privileged position.

Philosophy seems to be the one discipline that in principle claims to make judgments concerning all the rest. But this claim is not acknowledged, and even many philosophers themselves do not make it. Insofar as philosophy is a discipline that claims to understand all of reality, other disciplines must either bow to it or condemn it as guilty of intolerable arrogance. The fact that they do neither but merely make a modest place for it in the institution demonstrates the way in which pragmatic rather than theoretical criteria now govern educational judgments.

Thus, apart from any conscious philosophy or ideology, modern higher education is of its very nature naturalistic, in that no discipline can persuasively claim access to transcendent truth; secular, in that all disciplines are bound solely to "data" available to their practitioners; and rationalistic in a narrow sense, in that disciplinary activity is wholly limited to what can be learned cognitively and expressed in discursive formulas. In a very confused way, the student rebels around 1970 were asking if there was not more to education than this.

Thus the present crisis of the liberal arts was inevitable. Already perhaps fifty years ago, it was anomalous for institutions to prescribe certain courses as "essential to the educated man", since the working philosophies of most professors gave them no basis for making such a claim. The classical liberal arts survived almost entirely through tradition, or its cheap counterfeit inertia, and sooner or later were bound to be subjected to critical scrutiny. When academic radicals insist that there is no basis for erecting a hierarchy of disciplines, they are expressing a philosophic position but also merely stating a fact.

Whatever may be the case within a particular discipline, across disciplinary lines today no assertions can finally be either proven or rebutted, because the participants in the discussion lack common assumptions. (This does not prevent certain positions, for example, "multiculturalism", from becoming unquestionable dogmas, imposed essentially by coercion.)

But amidst the decay of higher education, there is little reason to suppose that there has been a collapse of standards in what have traditionally been called "the professions". Medical and law schools probably have stricter standards than they did thirty years ago and certainly require their students to imbibe far more information than they once did. Business has spawned advanced programs with more intellectual content—advanced economics, computer science—than the businessman of thirty years ago ever thought he needed. The physical sciences are probably more rigorous, and more spectacularly successful in their results, than ever. It is mainly in the relatively "soft" areas—the humanities and the misnamed social sciences—that there has been a fall into crises so profound that each discipline has great difficulty even justifying its own existence, and in which what were once considered unimpeachable "standards" (in English, for example, a knowledge of earlier versions of the language and an acquaintance with the works of canonical authors) have all but disappeared.

American universities are awash in vocationalism, a highly ironic development from the New Left revolution, which, in properly Marxist terms, condemned the way in which the universities had supposedly been "coopted" to the service of capitalism. There is, however, a straight line between the revolution of two decades ago and the deadening vocationalism of today. Student rebels of the earlier era demanded an end to all confining and arbitrary educational requirements, which meant the practical termination of the classical liberal arts. This was justified on the grounds that the students of that time were such free spirits that they wished to explore the mysteries of the cosmos in highly original and imaginative ways, so that even basic liberal arts courses were deadening. Even then it was apparent that most students, freed of the burden of liberal education, would use the available time to enroll in more and more "useful" courses. The classical university could defend itself against vocationalism by insisting that every student had to be broadly educated. Today it has no basis for saying this.

Possibly American higher education had by 1965 reached a peak of vitality it had never before attained, judging from such things as student intellectual achievements, the acceptance of genuine criteria of merit rather than mere social status by the elite schools, the professional competence of the faculty, and the seriousness with which the educational mission was almost universally taken. If that judgment is accurate, then this peak was attained immediately before the earthquake that has all but destroyed it.

Many faculty at the time found it expedient, for either cynical or foolishly idealistic motives, to praise the intellectual qualities of the student rebels, to the point of insisting that their assaults on the university were entirely wholesome, summoning those institutions back to the higher wisdom to which they were supposedly committed.

However, it was apparent even at the time that, with few exceptions, the most aggressive student rebels were not well educated even in subjects professedly dear to them, such as Marxist theory. Indeed, part of the New Left mystique was its contemptuous dismissal of any painstaking effort at acquiring knowledge on the grounds that the uncorrupted young possessed an almost X-ray vision into realities opaque to the older generation.

In an important way, the assault on the universities around 1970 was the victory of popular culture over high culture. The curriculum was "reformed" not after lengthy philosophical discussion of how wisdom and knowledge are acquired but solely because of the impatience of the students with anything felt to be an imposition on the self. Campuses became in effect privileged zones for unrestricted sex and drug use not after lengthy consideration of the mysteries of the human psyche as explored by any number of great thinkers but solely because of the urgent "needs" of adolescent bodies. Universities quasi-officially committed themselves to certain political stances—opposition to the Vietnam War, chiefly—not after study of the complexities of global politics and the morality of war but solely under the threat of campus violence and in response to slogans that could not have withstood a minute's rational analysis. As has often been pointed out, one factor in the student rebellion beginning around 1965 was the fact that young people of college age for the first time formed a major social class with abundant leisure and money and the ability to use both in ways that pleased them. They came to the universities already deeply formed by attitudes imbibed from films, television, and popular entertainment generally, attitudes impervious to almost any kind of reasoned appeal.

One of the many ironies of that era was the way in which the New Left met the Old Right on the common ground of philistinism. Fathers who were self-made businessmen had been sneered at for their coarse refusal to acknowledge cultural values higher than money. But their children, despite the benefits of the best secondary education, were equally crass in their refusal to acknowledge such values. The filthy speech movement at the University of California stood for more than simply the expansion of the acceptable "limits of discourse". It also was the victory of raw, assaultive acts against even a pretense of critical standards. The New Left in principle refused to argue its case, because to do so implied that "the establishment" might have a case of its own, and relied instead on naked assertions of the will, sustained by energies generated in the orgiastic depths of the youth culture.

The important question is not why the young of that era acted as they did but why their elders acted as they did, namely, abjectly surrendering to the worst of this philistine coercion, utterly failing to defend the principles to which they had professedly given their lives.

Cowardice and expediency alone do not explain this massive failure, nor was it peculiar to the universities, although it was most dramatic there. The youth culture could not have wreaked the havoc it did without the moral collapse of parents, clergy, political leaders, and almost every other kind of adult authority, who sometimes vied with one another in abasing themselves before their young critics.

The universities of 1965, apparently so proud and successful, in fact rested on a highly unstable synthesis that can be called classical modernism. In the secular institutions the battle with orthodox religion had long ago been won, and the universities had shown themselves hospitable, although for the most part in only a purely academic way, to every variety of modern thought—Marxism, Freudianism, positivism, the various forms of scepticism—having taken the idea of mere disciplinary professionalism as their one guiding truth.

From the modernist critique of the past, culminating at the end of the nineteenth century with Marx, Freud, Nietzsche, and Darwin, intellectuals of the midpart of this century thought they had constructed a viable synthesis, a balance between the corrosive acids of modernity and the need for some kind of social and cultural stability. The best representatives of this classical modernism were men such as Lionel Trilling and Jacques Barzun, who had given themselves entirely to the demands of modernity but had also evolved a new civility and sense of order, which has been called "the tradition of the new". Such people were rudely brushed aside by the New Left and by many of their own faculty colleagues, their desire to engage in civilized discussion itself regarded as a sign of moral weakness and a finicky defense of personal privilege.

In a sense the young radicals were right, because their assault on the intellectual citadels of classical modernism merely revealed the hollowness of that synthesis. In the end the classical modernist had no convincing argument to make against those who were, in a half-conscious way, allowing the acids of modernity to penetrate even more deeply into the psyche, a process that owed little to any great thinkers or great books and almost everything to a debased popular culture. If Freud was taken to mean total sexual hedonism, Marx to dictate violent assault on the bastions of privilege, Nietzsche the annihilation of all accepted beliefs, the classical modernists were hard put to argue that such interpretations were wholly wrong. Above all, they had no basis for even decreeing which positions might be right and which wrong, modernism itself, at whose altar they worshipped, having long ago destroyed the means of doing so. Many older persons around 1970 responded to the youth revolution with almost ecstatic approval because they saw there acted out the impulses that they had themselves entertained merely in theory for many years. They saw themselves as cowards who deserved the contempt their students heaped on them.

As noted, the parallel between the crises of university and church are very close, especially the fact that both institutions claim to embody a wisdom higher than the demands of ordinary life. University and church collapsed together, both to some extent willfully destroyed by their supposed guardians, the university being the very church that classical modernism had created, within which it thought that all people should in some way or other worship. But by 1970 neither church nor university could any longer identify what was to be regarded as sacred, what truth was capable of demanding people's unqualified allegiance.

For two centuries the heirs of the Enlightenment had been announcing the demise of classical Christianity, an announcement increasingly welcome within the precincts of the church also. When the rebellious young in effect announced the end of the Enlightenment itself, this announcement was greeted with cheers within that institution, which had attempted to enshrine that Enlightenment.

Although the student rebellion began at a state university,

that of California, its second manifestation was at an elite private institution—Columbia—and for the most part the private universities, including those supposedly imbued with a sense of tradition and gentility, did not fare any better than did the public institutions in those cultural wars. In many cases they probably fared worse, because openness to the New Left was the sign of a progressivism of which the private universities did not wish to be deprived.

All Catholic universities in 1965 were still relatively traditional. Most of their faculty and students were practicing Catholics, and required courses reflected this very clearly, especially in the dominance of scholastic philosophy. Rules of conduct were strict and strictly enforced. Given the fact that these schools had not as yet even experienced all the effects of classical modernism itself, it might have seemed that they were well situated to witness and to profit from the latter's ignominious demise. Instead, almost all Catholic institutions quickened their pace of change, so as to undergo in five years' time a cycle of decline that had taken the secular institutions more than a century to live through. Compared with the most "advanced" secular institutions today, most Catholic institutions are still somewhat conservative. But for the most part this is merely a matter of degree, and the gap is closing. (Most Catholic schools still have some required courses in theology and philosophy, for example. However, once the dogmatic principle has been discarded, it will be impossible for administrators, theologians, and philosophers to explain why such courses ought to be required. Eventually the proponents of total secularization will triumph, for the same reasons that the radicals triumphed in the secular schools twenty years ago.)

The dominance of vocationalism in today's universities is dictated by the simple fact that there is no other accepted principle by which educational achievement can be defended and enforced. If educators are honest, given their own assumptions, they cannot promise students that the educations they receive will be enlightening or liberating in the fullest sense, since to make such a promise is to imply absolute standards that have no defensible basis. Instead the universities in effect promise students lucrative employment after graduation, a promise that they can keep at least to some extent.

Put another way, as the dismal prospect of primary and secondary education shows even more dramatically than do the universities, it is impossible in the end to teach even purely secular and instrumental subjects without a transcendent purpose. The public schools are full of pupils impervious to learning because they can see no reason why they should allow any intrusion on the psychic worlds that have been spawned within them by the popular culture they imbibe from infancy. Meanwhile, Catholic schools are reported to be far more successful in convincing many of these same pupils that education does indeed have meaning.

The present morass of higher education cannot be overcome within the framework of education itself or of the universities as they now exist. Their plight is simply the inevitable end of a modernism whose more corrosive applications were discreetly kept out of sight for so long. Among other considerations, there cannot be a healthy university in a culture most of whose institutions are sick, nor can the university be expected to cure that pervasive illness.

Salvation even on the intellectual level can now spring only from religious conversion, from a complete turning of the mind and heart away from what is tyrannical and debilitating and toward what is freeing and inspiring. Only with this change of heart can modern people even be brought to understand the seriousness of their plight, much less the path out of it. Although some scholastic philosophers might believe otherwise, such success as traditional Catholic higher education had was always due in large measure to the religious vision of the reality that it imparted, which gave even purely rational pursuits a meaning they would not otherwise have had. (Perhaps the only successful effort at reforming a Catholic university in modern America has been the University of Steubenville, where the importance of religious conversion as the condition of everything else is obvious.)

Except in very rare cases (are there any aside from Steubenville?), it is unlikely that any Catholic universities in the United States will be reformed. The forces set in motion a quarter of a century ago are simply too strong to resist, even if some educational statesman were to take office determined to do so. Education among the ruins thus means the paradoxical decision to build new things for the sake of preserving what is eternal.

In certain ways colleges within colleges, such as the St. Ignatius Institute at the University of San Francisco, seem preferable. Such an arrangement gives students access to a variety of programs not available in small colleges and not excluding access to legitimate kinds of vocational training. Beyond this, students in such programs gain the valuable experience of having to cope with an indifferent or a hostile world as part of their actual educations. Under such conditions the effective participation of orthodox students in campus politics and campus media, as St. Ignatius students have done consistently, is excellent experience for life in the modern world.

But the vaunted pluralism of the modern university offers very few opportunities for such colleges within colleges. Thus the founding of new institutions, such as Christendom, St. Thomas Aquinas, and Thomas More College, is also dictated, and these too have distinct virtues. Among other things, they are almost by definition genuine communities in the fullest and most palpable sense, offering an education not only of the mind but also of the whole person, taking place in the midst of a group of dedicated individuals who witness their beliefs in their lives and not merely their lectures. Such an education was one of the recurrent demands of the New Left and, despite numerous "experimental" colleges at that time, seems to have been realized virtually nowhere, each such experiment foundering on the rock of ungoverned personal egos.

One of the ways in which some radical critics of twenty years ago were not wholly wrong was in asking whether schooling in a formal sense is necessarily the best way for all young people to achieve adulthood in modern society. Often the best students, in every respect, are those who have had some experience of the world, an experience that sometimes forces them to seek for truth in a pressingly personal way and thus makes them open both to religious conversion and to genuine education.

Although in the twentieth century the university has been the almost unquestioned center of intellectual activity in the United States, even to the point of swallowing so much of the artistic creativity that was once independent of any institution, there have been numerous times in the history of the West (the seventeenth and eighteenth centuries, notably) when the universities, for various reasons, did not have that importance. Today's universities will not soon lose either their prestige or their endowments. But in certain ways their intellectual and spiritual bankruptcy, the depressing monolith of their pervasive leftist ideologies, has rendered them irrelevant to the intellectual tasks of the age. This is immediately obvious in the fact that many of the people who are actually thinking about today's world and its needs are now associated with "think tanks" and other institutions outside the regular academic structure. If degrees are in a sense no longer important except for purposes of employment, those alternative institutions may in some ways begin to assume educational functions on behalf of young people interested in real learning. There has also been a proliferation of journals, publishing houses, and professional organizations that are conscious alternatives to existing institutions.

If popular culture has indeed defeated high culture, as seems to have happened in the universities of two decades ago, the problem of popular culture will have to be addressed in some serious and effective ways. There is a paradox here in that those with the principles and beliefs necessary to redeem popular culture are generally those most in ignorance of it because of its often disgusting, and always shallow, character. But the redemption of popular culture cries out for attention.

One of the numerous ironies of the present age is that, as
the myth that American Catholics came of age with John F.
Kennedy is finally being exposed, a genuine Catholic coming
of age has been all but overlooked. During the Reagan administration particularly, certain individuals such as William
Bennett attracted a great deal of attention, much of it sym-
pathetic, through their willingness to speak boldly on behalf
of such basic truths as self-discipline and the integrity of the
family, drawing on the roots of their own Catholic educations
(at least at the secondary level) of three decades ago. On the
Supreme Court, Justices Antonin Scalia and Anthony Kennedy
may bring similar educations to bear on the great disputed ques-
tions of the day. Part of the irony, however, is that the leading
spokesmen for Catholic education do not see in such persons
the fulfillment and vindication of their efforts but the reverse—
Catholic education has so immersed itself in the surrounding
secular morass that men such as Bennett, Scalia, and Kennedy
are often treated like embarrassing atavisms, reminders of a past
that professional Catholic educators are trying to forget.

Church leaders do not seem to understand what many Catholic educators understand very well—that, as Cardinal Newman
warned would be the case, the university functions as a rival
church, pitting the dogmas of relativism against the dogmatic
teachings of revealed religion. Most Catholic educators have
resolved this dilemma simply by declaring that it is no dilemma
—they have turned the Catholic universities themselves into rival churches, essentially promoting the same secularist agenda.

But the Church as a whole can still be a great teaching force
—through the pulpit, through the Catholic press, above all
through bold and articulate religious leaders able to capture
the popular imagination and win people's hearts. As the loss
of the Catholic universities finally becomes undeniable, the
Church must use her creative abilities to develop new ways of
teaching both Catholics and the larger world the truths of the
Faith and of entering in a vigorous way into the great debates
of the age. (It is tragic that the Vatican's apparent concession

of autonomy to the American Catholic universities serves no
other purpose than to enable those institutions to continue to
claim the Catholic name for the decade or so during which
they still may wish to claim it. It is unlikely that, much after
the year 2000, many faculty will glory in that name, and it is
unlikely that administrators and trustees will continue to insist
on it.)

Allan Bloom's celebrated critique of American educational
illness, *The Closing of the American Mind*,[1] offers as acute a diag-
nosis as can be made of the nature of the disease. His proffered
cures seem by contrast very pallid and are open precisely to
the attacks already made on the classical modernist synthesis.

At certain times in history the patient voices of cool ratio-
nality are highly persuasive, and in those ages great syntheses,
such as that of St. Thomas Aquinas, are forged. But in ages of
fragmentation and decay, of strife and despair, only the boldest
and most prophetic voices are heard. Believing Christians are
by far the people best qualified to speak with convincing authority at this juncture of history, and it appears that on most
matters—the "life issues", church and state, the nature of truth
itself—evangelical Protestants must turn to Catholics for the
intellectual resources that they need to carry their positions
beyond sectarian dogma. In the years ahead some will follow
the venerable monastic vocation of patiently storing up the
fragments of culture against a better day. But for most, God's
will and the needs of humanity at this time in history seem
to require a role more akin to that of the apostles on the first
Pentecost.

NOTES

[1] Allan Bloom, *The Closing of the American Mind* (Beaverton, Or.: Touchstone Books, 1988).

ROBERT A. GEORGE

ACADEMIC FREEDOM:
THE GROUNDS FOR
TOLERATING ABUSES

We are all familiar—indeed, all too familiar—with abuses of academic freedom. Consider, for example, the following two cases.

A controversy currently raging in this city of controversies concerns a City University of New York (CUNY) professor named Leonard Jeffries whose lectures frequently degenerate into racist and anti-Semitic diatribes. Professor Jeffries, who is black, asserts that whites are "ice people" who are prone to cruelty and violence, while blacks are "sun people" who are inclined to compassion and peace. He attributes the racial superiority of blacks to whites to the presence in black skin of the pigment melanin. Jeffries also claims that the slave trade was "financed by Jews" and alleges that "a financial system of destruction of black people" has been put into place as part of "a conspiracy, planned and plotted and programmed out of Hollywood [by] people called Greenberg and Weisberg and Trigliani".[1] The publication of these remarks has produced a chorus of demands that CUNY dismiss or at least discipline Jeffries. The professor and his supporters, however, maintain that he enjoys a moral and legal immunity from such actions as a matter of academic freedom.

In the early 1980s, a controversy erupted in Catholic circles when it was reported that George N. Gordon, the Chairman of the Communications Department at Fordham University, was contributing opinion pieces to an obscene (and viciously anti-Catholic) weekly called *Screw* magazine. (In those days, it was still unclear whether a member of the faculty could get away with this sort of thing at an ostensibly Catholic institution. The situation has since been clarified.) In any event, when Fordham's President was pressed to take action to combat the scandal of having a member of its faculty writing in *Screw*, he observed that Gordon's writings "could and would be defended as a right of academic freedom".[2]

Now, when I cite the cases of Jeffries and Gordon as "abuses" of academic freedom, I do not mean to assert that their legal and moral claims to immunity from disciplinary action on grounds of academic freedom are invalid. To render such a judgment, I would need more detailed information about the cases than is currently in my possession. I am interested in the cases of Jeffries and Gordon because they clearly involve abuses of academic freedom *even if* their claims to immunity from disciplinary action on grounds of academic freedom turn out to be valid.

I am considering here a certain possibility that will perhaps strike the reader as paradoxical. By describing the activities of Jeffries and Gordon as "abuses", I am suggesting that these activities are wrong. But if it is wrong for Jeffries to teach bigotry and for Gordon to publish in *Screw*, then Jeffries has no right to teach bigotry and Gordon has no right to publish in *Screw*. If the professors in question have no right to do what they have done, then how can their activities be subjects of valid claims to immunity from disciplinary action on grounds of academic freedom? How can they have a right not to be disciplined for doing things that they have no right to do? Does the right to academic freedom include rights to do wrongs?

Let me contrast two very different understandings of the value of academic freedom. Each of these understandings is part of a broader understanding of political morality and the value of freedom. On either understanding, there will sometimes be conclusive reasons for tolerating what I have called abuses of academic and other freedoms. The moral grounds of such toleration, however, differ sharply, reflecting the profound difference between the two understandings regarding the value of freedom.

According to one understanding, the value of academic freedom, and more generally of freedom of speech, is in the self-expression of feelings and opinions. Proponents of this understanding claim that people do indeed have certain moral rights to do moral wrongs. It is wrong, they say, for the state to interfere with or punish free expression, or for the university to prevent or discipline faculty for abuses of academic freedom, because to do so is to violate a right to free expression that holds even where one's act of expression is morally wrong. The moral ground of the obligation of the state or of university authorities not to act against the speaker is precisely the speaker's moral right to express what he feels or believes even where, from the moral point of view, that expression of feeling or opinion is wrong.[3]

This view of freedom is associated with contemporary "anti-perfectionist"[4] liberalism and informs the approach to these matters typically taken by the American Civil Liberties Union and like-minded advocacy groups. Proponents of this view might apply it to the Jeffries case as follows: Leonard Jeffries is morally wrong to preach racial hatred and anti-Semitism. Nevertheless, he has a moral right to express himself as he pleases, even where what he says is wrong and even where he is morally wrong to say it. Because Jeffries has this right, it would be wrong for CUNY to take action against him. A liberal Catholic might offer a similar analysis of the Gordon case: George Gordon was wrong to write for *Screw* magazine. Still, he has a right to express himself in the forum of his choice, even where his choice of forum is immoral. Because it would be a violation of this right for Fordham to take action against him, the President of Fordham was right to abstain from taking action.

Now for the alternative understanding. According to this understanding, the value of academic freedom, and more generally freedom of speech,[5] is in the pursuit of truth. The freedom to inquire, speak, publish, debate, and so forth is valuable as a means or condition for the creation and authentic appropriation of knowledge, for its preservation, and for its transmission to others. Proponents of this understanding share with those who hold the first understanding the view that that valuable academic freedom requires, within limits, the creation of immunities from constraints and sanctions for the expression of opinion. And they recognize that the immunities that are essential to the creation and maintenance of an environment or milieu of freedom in which the truth can be vigorously pursued will be subject to abuse. The moral ground of the toleration of abuses, however, is not in a putative right of the abuser to self-expression. Rather, toleration of abuse has a point, and is required, only in those circumstances in which prudence dictates restraint from interference with professorial wrongdoing for the sake of preserving a milieu that encourages the vigorous and unabashed pursuit of truth.

Here the reader may perceive another paradox. How can concern for the truth provide the ground for tolerating the expression and dissemination of falsehood? Indeed, doesn't concern for the truth provide a conclusive reason to prevent the expression and dissemination of untruth? If the value of academic freedom and freedom of speech is grounded in the intrinsic value of truth, why not take the view that the scope of academic freedom and freedom of speech is precisely and only the freedom to say and teach what is.

Why accord error any rights? For the truth to be humanly valuable, it must be authentically appropriated by human beings. The authentic appropriation of truth and its secure contemplation require vital inquiry and reflection, genuine understanding and judgment. The freedom necessary for the authentic pursuit of truth and its real appropriation entails the freedom to get it wrong. The milieu of freedom necessary for vigorous inquiry and debate requires a measure of immunity from interference with teaching and publication that simply cannot be rendered inconsistent with the possibility of abuse. The spirit of inquiry that is essential to the authentic appropriation of truth is easily suffocated where there is no freedom. Thus, authorities in academic institutions and elsewhere who love truth will, precisely for the sake of truth, preserve and protect freedom of inquiry even at the price of tolerating error and abuse. Such authorities recognize that error and abuse are truly "lesser evils", lesser threats to truth, than the inauthenticity and corruption that flourish in the absence of freedom and that gravely impede the disinterested pursuit of truth and jeopardize its secure possession by scholars and students.

Is this to suggest that the alternative view—let us call it "the correct view"—also shares with the liberal view of academic freedom belief in moral rights to do moral wrongs? No. The correct view understands the duty to tolerate those abuses that should be tolerated as grounded not in the rights of the abuser but rather in the obligation to maintain a milieu of freedom on which scholars of goodwill can rely (and that rascals will, alas, exploit) for the sake of the common good of the academic community in the pursuit and secure enjoyment of truth. Within limits, error and even abuse must be tolerated precisely for the sake of the common good of truth.

The rights of a Leonard Jeffries or a George Gordon, if their claims to immunity on the ground of academic freedom are valid, are not, under the correct view, a *ground* of the immunities they claim. Rather, these immunities, considered from the claimant's point of view (and thus expressible in the language of rights), are rights that "shadow" duties *grounded independently* in prudential judgments that the common good of the academic community of CUNY or Fordham is served best, here and now at least, by refraining from disciplinary actions that are likely to damage the common interest of members of the university in a milieu of freedom appropriate to truth-seeking. If on this occasion CUNY should tolerate the bigotry of Leonard Jeffries or Fordham should tolerate the obscenity of George Gordon, it is not because their rights to academic freedom include the rights to preach bigotry or publish in obscene magazines; and if, contrary to the demands of prudence (let us suppose), the university authorities take action against a Jeffries or Gordon, the wrong done consists not in a violation of individual rights as such but in the damaging of a community interest in academic freedom. If there is injustice in the taking of such action, Jeffries and Gordon are not its victims.

Of course, advocates of the liberal view will be quick to point out that their theory will more sharply and securely limit the authority of officials to interfere with or punish abuses of academic freedom or freedom of speech. Their theory comes nearer to an absolutism of free speech and academic freedom than does the alternative theory. Advocates of the correct understanding, however, will see no reason to count this observation as a point against them. They will argue that their theory grounds the value of academic freedom in an intelligible human good, for example, truth, rather than in a mere human capacity, for example, self-expression, which is valuable when exercised well and valueless or worse when exercised badly.[6] And they will observe that their approach avoids the extravagant hypothesis that people sometimes have a moral right to do moral wrong.

The subject of these brief reflections has been academic freedom, its ground and the ground for sometimes tolerating abuses. I have argued that the correct view of the matter understands academic freedom as a value that serves the good of truth. The establishment and maintenance of a milieu conducive to the vigorous pursuit of truth and its secure contemplation require academic freedom, but academic freedom is not all that is required. An atmosphere properly conducive to truth-seeking must be imbued by a love of the truth—not just as an instrumental good but also as something worthwhile for its own sake, as an intrinsic and irreducible aspect of human well-being and fulfillment. The greatest danger to truth-seeking on many campuses today is posed by the phenomenon of "political correctness", which not only establishes an orthodoxy in discussions in which orthodoxy has no place but also, more insidiously, treats knowledge as a mere instrumental good to be manipulated in the service of political ends.

Finally, I would like to offer a word about Catholic universities. In such universities, there should be a special dedication to truth as a human good and a divine gift. The atmosphere of Catholic institutions should be imbued above all with a desire to know the truth about God. Even with respect to theological inquiry, however, a due regard for academic freedom will sometimes require the prudent toleration of abuses. Still, there are limits to what may legitimately be counted as Catholic theology, and these limits are established by the authoritative teachings of the Magisterium. From the point of view of the Catholic Faith, these are truths we firmly possess. The role of the theologian, as I understand it, is to explain, illuminate, and develop the implications of these truths in the service of the Church. A milieu conducive to the fulfillment of these responsibilities by theologians functioning as scholars and teachers will, to be sure, require academic freedom; it will also crucially depend, however, on the prevalence of valid assumptions as to the authoritative source of truths of Faith without which the integrity of Catholic theology is hopelessly compromised.

NOTES

[1] *New York Times*, Aug. 7, 1991, p. B1.

[2] *National Review*, Sept. 20, 1985, p. 9.

[3] This view is ably defended by Jeremy Waldron in "A Right to Do Wrong", *Ethics* 92 (1981): 21–39. It is criticized with equal skill by William Galston in "On the Alleged Right to Do Wrong: A Reply to Waldron", *Ethics* 93 (1983): pp. 320–24.

[4] "Antiperfectionism" in legal and political philosophy is the view that governments have an obligation to remain neutral on the controversial question of what counts as a morally good life. Influential antiperfectionist liberal theories have been adumbrated in contemporary philosophy by John Rawls in *A Theory of Justice* (Cambridge, Mass.: Harvard University Press, 1971) and Ronald Dworkin in *A Matter of Principle* (Cambridge, Mass.: Harvard University Press, 1985). For powerful criticisms of antiperfectionism, see John Finnis, *Natural Law and Natural Rights* (Oxford: Clarendon Press, 1980), and Joseph Raz, *The Morality of Freedom* (Oxford: Clarendon Press, 1986).

[5] The eminent political theorist Harvey Mansfield, Jr. distinguishes more sharply than I think is warranted between free speech, whose purpose, he says, "is to make democratic government possible", and academic freedom, whose purpose "is to further inquiry". "Political Correctness and the Suicide of the Intellect", *The Heritage Lectures* 337 (1991), p. 4. Free speech is, to be sure, valuable as a means to good government; but it is also valuable as a condition for the cooperative pursuit, discovery, and transmission of truth.

[6] In this respect, "self-expression" is like "autonomy", that is, it is valuable when exercised for morally good ends, but valueless (or worse) when exercised immorally. On the conditional value of autonomy, see Raz, *The Morality of Freedom*, pp. 381 and 411.

JUDE P. DOUGHERTY

STAYING CATHOLIC

The first thing to recognize about Catholic higher education is that its demand begins in the nursery. It is in the preschool years that the child first encounters the tangible fruits of baptism. Those fruits are encountered in the symbols found in the home, in the grace said at mealtime, in parental encouragement of night prayers, in Bible story coloring books, and in the Sunday morning trek to the parish church. Assuming committed parents, the child is brought through successive years to the practice and understanding of his Faith. Practice and understanding are inseparable, and practice obviously depends on understanding, but in the early years, habituated behavior is the prelude to intellectual quest. Aristotle could have said that habits perform the same function in religious matters as they do in other aspects of life. Though in ancient Greece the father determined which gods were to be worshipped, mothers no doubt were then, as they are still, the major tutors in matters of the Faith.

One may ask, why is the Faith so prized that it is preserved and passed along, sometimes with great sacrifice of time and of resource and, in the past, often defended with the sword? Why do Catholic parents, even in a time of uncertainty within the Church, seek a Catholic education for their offspring? From France to Indonesia the battle is the same, the preservation of Catholic education against the tendency of the state to usurp all tutelage.

What is it that the Catholic mind seeks to preserve? What is it that the Faith brings to one's life? "Understanding", answered

Augustine. But the Faith is not merely a set of intellectual insights. It entails a morality, a way of acting, a way of behaving, a way of celebrating. One's faith both presupposes and identifies one with a community of believers. One is by faith a member of a religious body. Those who profess the Catholic Faith recognize that it comes to them not merely as the fulfillment of Hebrew prophecies, not simply as a result of the teaching of Christ and his apostles, but as a result of teaching by a Magisterium instituted by Christ himself. Christ founded a Church out of love for the very race whose redemption he secured by his sacrificial death on the Cross. That Church brings to mankind not only essential teachings regarding the nature and purpose of human life but also the sacraments, which bless and restore an ever frail human nature.

Christ did not invent religion; religion is found wherever man has acknowledged a transcendent order. Ancient peoples described in the Bible worshipped their gods. So too did the Greeks and Romans, often in elaborate and noble ceremony. From antiquity, mankind has celebrated through religious ceremony the important passages of life—birth, puberty, marriage, death, and the seasons of the year. The Church has absorbed and reconsecrated, and in some instances redirected, the fruit of natural religion, often standing alone in defense of truths and practices that even the pre-Christian acknowledged.

To say these things is to say why the Church is loved. She brings light, she provides joy and solace, and she interrupts the humdrum with feast, in some countries more often than in others. She is positioned to show the way; she makes available the Eucharist, in whose presence many a soul has found not only tranquility but also speculative and practical wisdom. The Church's mission necessarily leads to activity in the practical order. Apart from her sacramental function, her most important task is education.

To speak of Catholic education is to acknowledge, for one thing, a specific telos to education and, for another a distinctive Tradition. The recognition of that telos is, of course, shared by other believers. It consists in the awareness that the grave is not the end of man; that man is called to a life in union with the divine; that a life, whatever else it might be, consists in knowledge and love of God. Acknowledgment of this transcendent end colors the whole of education. At no stage is ultimate fulfillment confused with terrestrial happiness.

The distinctive feature of Catholic education is the Catholic Tradition itself, a very complex Tradition spanning two thousand years of history. One need only enter the Basilica of St. Ambrose in Milan to have the historical asserted. There, under the high altar, lie the remains of Ambrose, who died in 397, accompanied by the remains of St. Gervase and St. Protase, both first-century martyrs.

That physical continuity is a visible reminder of intellectual inheritance. Ambrose taught Augustine, and Augustine taught the West. The Fathers, no less than the Greeks and Romans upon whom they drew, were educators. From Augustine's *De Magistra* to Newman's *Idea of a University*, one can find scores of books, some of them Christian and literary classics, that speak to the aims of education. In common they recognize that the end of life is contemplation and that the road to the Beatific Vision requires a kind of interiority even in the midst of the crassest of temporal pursuits.

A full Catholic life is a life of the intellect, but a life of the intellect under certain conditions: the intellect drawing upon its experience of the present, certainly, but experience understood and interpreted within the context of an appropriated past. Christ himself is the model. In teaching he appealed to his listeners' grasp of nature and built upon the inherited. Christ came to proclaim a new law, but in doing so was respectful of the best of ancient codes. His disciples found him credible. When St. John Chrysostom sought an empirical proof for the existence of God, he found it in the splendor of the Church herself. The evidence that he found compelling came from the fact that the Church in her teaching appealed to noble and low, rich and poor, learned and not, and had through her teaching in a brief span transformed for the good the lives of countless individuals and even of nations. An institution that produced such good effects, he reasoned, could only have a divine origin.

Three things I wish to underscore: the requirement of critical intelligence, the need for learning, and the need for the Church. Unaided intelligence will not suffice. Isolated from tradition and from community, it will become as sterile as Hume's believer, sequestered in a private meditation for a moment in the confines of his study. Just as a knowledge of the practical arts is required for success in most of life's activities, so too in matters of religious activity is learning required. It would be foolish to proceed as if God and the way to God were unknown. Religion is a communal activity. The acknowledgment of God's existence, the acknowledgment of man's debt to him, and an awareness of the propriety of paying that debt are communal affairs. Awareness of the need to worship is found wherever men are found. Piety is thus a natural virtue. *Spirituality* is but a term for the lifting of intellect and will to things divine. It is a habit of referral, grounded in contemplation, a habit of understanding things in the light of their finality.

The love of God requires some knowledge of God. No one can love an unknown God. God has to be present in some manner before his goodness can command the volitional act. Awareness is the result of some effort on our part, the result of our attentiveness to a witness, be it oral or written. The normal channel of awareness is parental teaching reinforced by formal education. Formal education can carry us to the heights of theological speculation, but the basic truths that ground appreciation are simple and are available to the whole of mankind. There are degrees of knowledge, and there are degrees of appreciation. Natural knowledge is complemented by revelation, and he who hears and is privileged to possess the best of human knowledge can advance without limit. Development is open ended. Like science, the augmentation of a knowledge of things divine profits from concerted effort. Rational disputation is social. Most of those we take as guides to the devout life were learned people. They made use of both native intelligence and learning to ferret out the secrets of the divine. St. John of the Cross and his modern disciples such as Edith Stein and Karol Wojtyla come immediately to mind.

To describe the beauty of the Church is not to claim that that beauty is universally acknowledged. A scepticism with respect to Christian convictions has been forming among the Occidental intelligentsia for the last century and a half. Nietzsche observed already in the last century that Western culture no longer possessed the spiritual resources that had justified its existence and without which he felt it could not survive.

What is more recent is that this loss of moral sense has now made itself felt on the level of the common man. In more ways than one, we are children of the Enlightenment. Views entertained in eighteenth- and nineteenth-century drawing rooms and in the academy of that day have in our own lifetime entered the marketplace. Voltaire urged the eradication of Christianity from the world of higher culture, but he was willing to have it remain in the stables and in the scullery lest a servant class, deprived of a moral outlook, might steal. Mill repudiated Christianity but not the religion of humanity, which he thought to be, from the point of view of the state, a useful thing. Comte was more benevolent in his attitude toward Christian practice. In spite of his denial of all metaphysical validity to religious belief, he was willing to accept as a civic good the moral and ritual traditions of Catholic Christianity. Durkheim was not so positive. For him, a major task of the state is to free individuals from partial societies such as the family, religious organizations, and labor and professional groups. Modern individualism, Durkheim thought, depends on preventing the absorption of individuals into secondary or mediating groups.

On this side of the Atlantic, many of these ideas were to find twentieth-century expression in the philosophy of John Dewey. In his philosophy of education, Dewey had no use for religion or religious institutions, whatever roles they may have played in the past. Religion, he thought, is an unreliable source for knowledge and, in spite of contentions to the contrary, even motivation. Many of the values held dear by the religious are worthy of consideration and should not be abandoned, but a proper rationale ought to be sought for those deemed commendable. Through his critique of religion, Dewey sought not merely to eliminate the church from political influence but also to eliminate it as an effective agent in private life. Religion is deemed socially dangerous insofar as it gives practical credence to a divine law and attempts to mold personal or social conduct in conformity with norms that look beyond temporal society.

An awareness of American intellectual history is not irrelevant. At the turn of the century, at the very time many ideas characteristic of the Enlightenment were finding adherents in the academic mainstream, the schools themselves were changing hands. Toward the end of the nineteenth century and the beginning of the twentieth, the land grant colleges were coming into being. Lacking religious sponsorship or identity, they tended to reflect the secular spirit. At the same time the older Protestant-founded colleges were losing their denominational identity. Whereas in the last quarter of the nineteenth century nearly every major chair of philosophy was held by an idealist whose philosophy was a support for Christianity, by 1910 the situation was reversed. Nearly every chair was held by a naturalist. The causes for the shift are complex. Any explanation would have to take note of the widespread confidence placed in the methods of the sciences, social theories emanating from Europe, the discoveries of Darwin, and in the kind of biblical scholarship that tended to place doubt on the uniqueness of Christianity. Though these ideas did not have immediate social or cultural effects, the academy became cut off from its Christian parentage, coming to construe itself as a critic of established institutions, not as the bearer of a tradition or culture. Science was identified with "critical" intelligence. Its methods were to be turned on everything heretofore considered sacrosanct. It took another generation or two before such a critique was to reach the primary and secondary schools.

Until the close of the Second World War, the common schools were largely Protestant. Since the beginning of the republic, their Protestant character was evident and taken for granted. It was because of Catholic dissatisfaction with Protestant public schools that the parochial school system came into being. That dissatisfaction plus the massive immigration of the second half of the nineteenth century made a dual educational system possible. But in the post–World War II period, the Protestant character of the public schools began to change. The secular philosophy of the academy began to make itself felt through a series of Supreme Court decisions. The Court had always appealed to the antiestablishment claims of the First Amendment, but it was now reading into the amendment outlooks that the Founding Fathers did not press and that would probably have been contradictory to the views of most. In the 1947 *Everson v. Board of Education* decision, Justice Black decreed: "The establishment of religion clause of the First amendment means at least this. . . . No tax in any amount, large or small, can be levied to support any religious activities or institutions, whatever they may be called, or whatever form they may adopt to teach or practice religion."[1]

Though *Everson* upheld bus rides for parochial school children, those hostile to religion were to quote it time and again. *McCullum* (1948) declared illegal religious education in public school buildings, *Engle v. Vitale* (1962) struck down prayer, *Abington School District v. Schempp* (1963) outlawed Bible reading, and the *Committee for Public Education v. Nyquist* (1976) ruled illegal tuition reimbursement arrangements.

In thirty years, these decisions of the Court were, in effect, to secularize public education. Whereas the schools previously fostered basic Christian values through their traditions of common prayer, Bible reading, textbooks such as the McGuffy reader, and the celebration of religious feasts, those values ceased explicitly to be fostered. To be sure, the Court did not prohibit the teaching about religion or the reading of Sacred Scripture as a form of literature, but there is no doubt that Protestant Christianity was not only challenged but also removed as a positive influence. Many observers have found that a nondenominational Protestantism has merely been replaced by a secular humanism, which, while not a religion, is clearly an ideology with consequences for social policy and personal moral behavior.

Significant, too, is the Court's refusal, despite its decision in *Pierce v. The Society of Sisters* (1925) acknowledging the prior parental right to educate the child, to allow options with respect to schools unless parents are willing and able to pay tuition in a nonstate school.

Christopher Dawson, commenting on the American system, has said, "The secular state school is an instrument of the Enlightenment."[2] Insofar as the state preempts education, the schools have become the seats of a new ideology, the ideology of secularism. Leo Pfeffer argues that a secular "state requires a secular state school". He assures us that "the secularization of the state does not mean the secularization of society".[3] But this opinion, as Walter Berns has pointed out, was not shared by Rousseau, for example, or by Washington; Jefferson too had his doubts. Experience can be no guide here because we have no experience of living under wholly secular auspices. It is only in our day that we have approximated the secular state, a state that not only forbids aid to religion but in the United States and elsewhere is also under constant pressure to sever the connection between law and morality that finds its origins in religious doctrine. To quote Walter Berns, "If Pfeffer should prove wrong when he says that 'society' can remain religious though the state be indifferent to religion", it will be left to our descendants to determine "whether de Tocqueville was right when he said that unlike despotism, liberty cannot govern without faith".[4] Other decisions of the Court reflecting a secular outlook have permitted, in the name of freedom, the widespread introduction of pornography, the abortion decision, and the casting aside of those conventions of decency that used to govern public discourse. It is unfortunate that in recent years public opinion has inevitably begun to follow the Court. America, unfortunately, is a conformist society in which it is difficult for an individual or a social group to maintain separate standards of value or independent ways of life. The state's near monopoly on education and the uniformity encouraged by the media have produced decisive changes in American society.

This scenario would suggest that if religious literacy is to be achieved, it will be achieved without help from and sometimes against the interference of the state. If it were once true, as de Tocqueville reported, that all Americans regard religion as indispensable to the maintenance of republican institutions, that claim cannot be made today.

Unfortunately, Catholic institutions themselves have not escaped the drift toward secularism. Some have modeled themselves after the secular state school; many have surrendered ties with ecclesiastical bodies in an attempt to qualify for state funding. Others have counseled what they believe to be a prudent course for Catholic colleges and universities vis-à-vis state and federal regulations, advising administrators not to pursue a distinctively Catholic course but to seek objectives only insofar as they seem consonant with legal trends. A too-Catholic student body, an effort to maintain Catholic identity through a predominantly Catholic faculty, are regarded as invitations to hostile rulings on the part of the courts when determining eligibility for federal funds and tax-exempt status.

While conflict should not be invited, Catholic educators must realize that certain issues inevitably have to be faced on the basis of principle. Catholic educators can elect to surrender, or they can maintain policies that wisdom would dictate and that still have the support of the people and legislative bodies, though perhaps not of the courts and the secular elite that the courts tend to follow.

The Church's need for an educated class has never been greater. To produce that class, her own centers will have to be maintained and brought to high standards. While in many respects scholarship is a highly personal endeavor, individual effort requires institutional support. Scholars require like-minded colleagues and supporting disciplines. Moreover, the kind of inquiry most needed by the Church is not likely to be carried out in any programmatic way within a secular institution. True, individuals in many major state or private institutions contribute to the intellectual life of the Church, and their contributions are indispensable. But their individual work is not the same as a program or an institution, nor can they create single-handedly the intellectual milieu in which Catholic studies flourish.

To deal with the secular mind without succumbing, one needs not only the Faith, but also sound and careful training in philosophy and theology. The essence of secularity is the conviction that there is no evidence for the existence of God. The secular outlook deprives belief of a rational foundation and, consequently, of its credibility. Accommodated by the unwary, it results in a fideist Christianity, which eschews the intellectual force of tradition. The result is a radical evangelical fundamentalism with little intellectual credibility. Catholicism has not been handicapped in the same fashion. Its appreciation of classical learning has enabled it to deal with the findings of modern science and with the attacks brought by various forms of scepticism and positivism without slipping into fideism.

The Catholic world-view is woven out of threads that are cultural and philosophical as well as biblical and theological, strands provided by Greece and Rome as well as by Jerusalem. The appropriation of this Tradition requires centers of learning where these components and their attendant disciplines, especially history and languages, are represented in a competent and significant way. There is no shortcut to wisdom, and no substitute for it. Social science cannot replace history and philosophy. Learning theory or clinical psychology is no substitute for metaphysics. Courses offered under titles such as "Population Problems", "Human Ecology", and "Group Behavior" ought to supplement, not drive out, Greek and Roman History or the History of Medieval Civilization. In the last decades, the tendency to substitute the social and behavioral sciences for traditional disciplines has accelerated. This has had a detrimental effect for two reasons. One, the social sciences come laden with conclusions relying on assumptions that take a very sophisticated mind to evaluate, but the social science courses have most often been substituted for the philosophy that would render that necessary evaluation possible. A second reason is the value of their conclusions to the moral sciences. There is little knowledge gained from contemporary social science of the sort bearing on fundamental moral issues that was not also available in antiquity. Basic moral truths and principles did not have to await the nineteenth century for discovery. But the student is left with the impression that everything is in flux and that all that is important was discovered in his lifetime.

A further issue is the activist direction some training takes. The heavy emphasis on social service and counseling at the expense of other disciplines represents an imbalance. True, the Church's mission includes both the pastoral and the prophetic, but in an age when the state has undertaken massively to care for the poor, the sick, and the aged through its almost omnipresent welfare programs, it is foolish to emphasize the social when the prophetic or intellectual leadership of the Church is much in demand.

Another propensity that ought to be reexamined is the tendency to substitute techniques of counseling for first-order learning. Much of the personal malaise encountered in the pastoral order is the direct outcome of social ills that have to be addressed at the roots. As Dawson once remarked, the secular leviathan is vulnerable only at its brain. Only through its intellectuals will the Church be able to counteract the philosophical and ideological forces behind the secular movement. Clearly, it is more important to influence the king than to shelter the beggar. There are fewer in need of "counseling" when properly directed social structures are in order. Judging from some Church-sponsored programs, contemporary Catholics seem more bent on picking up the pieces than in turning off the engine of destruction.

A university community is not unlike the human body in that self-maintenance is possible only within a narrow range of conditions. Body temperature may vary within a few degrees, but no more than that; atmospheric pressure does not leave much room for dalliance, whether above or below the earth. We are assuming, of course, that the university really has specifiable goals and that it seeks to maintain itself in being.

At the heart of a university are both the people who compose it and the principles by which they choose to regulate their activity. In making appointments, it is foolish not to take into consideration the intellectual fabric and the moral character of a candidate for faculty membership. When a scholar becomes a member of a university faculty, he becomes part of a collegium, a collegium that he will in due course come to influence, whose tone he will help to establish. Both Plato and Aristotle taught the unity of the virtues. If a man is devoid of courage, there will be occasions when he will betray the ideals of the group. If he does not have his passions under control, his actions will in time affect his productivity and reliability.

Defects in perspective show up as the years go by. The young assistant professor who in the beginning of his career may make his contribution primarily through teaching will in due course be called to membership on committees and governing boards not only within a department but in the university and perhaps in the community as well. If his own perceptions or fundamental outlook differs from those of the sponsoring body, he will inevitably contribute to the changing of the official outlook. Examples are not hard to find. If he personally is not convinced of the value of a liberal education, specifically of the need to study languages, and to know history, philosophy, and theology, these convictions will manifest themselves as he votes on institutional policy. Similarly, the relaxed attitude of some in sexual matters will influence their vote on policies governing student life.

One of the most valuable analyses of higher education to emerge in recent decades is that of A. McIntyre, whose *Three Rival Versions of Moral Inquiry*[5] points to the almost irreconcilable difference between an educational institution based on the principles of Enlightenment philosophy and one grounded in the thought of St. Thomas. Catholics for decades have acted as if the parts of a Catholic and a secular institution are interchangeable, not noticing that the compliment was not reciprocated. Higher education, McIntyre points out, has no shared set of principles on which judgment may be based. In the absence of a shared inheritance, there is no common universe of discourse. The contemporary American university, unaware of its own Enlightenment bias, has excluded rival modes of inquiry, including the Catholic intellectual Tradition. McIntyre does not despair that rival modes can enter into dialogue, but the condition of fruitful exchange is the acknowledgment of fundamental difference and the need for integrity in discourse. There can be no ecumenism in the realm of ideas. One cannot affirm and deny at the same time and in the same respect. Where the truths of the Catholic Faith are denied, there is no point in glossing over that fact. Acceptance of those truths leads the believer down one intellectual path, denial down another. Only when this is recognized can there be an honest exchange. To be Catholic is to be different.

Writing in the 1960s, John Courtney Murray made a rather somber assessment of American cultural trends. He had more confidence in the Church to provide the necessary leadership than he had in American institutions. Time has proven that his fears were not groundless. Writers as diverse as Walker Percy and John Neuhaus have proclaimed the Catholic moment. But if the salvific teaching is to come, it will come only from trained Catholic minds. To prepare them, Catholic institutions for higher learning are indispensable. To reinforce them where they exist, to recover them where they are wavering, we need, first of all, the kind of assessment attempted here. Then we need men and women of courage who are willing to shoulder responsibility in the interest of long-range goals. Etienne Gilson once remarked that the trouble with us Catholics is that we are not proud enough of the Faith. I hope that cannot be said about many of us.

NOTES

[1] *Everson v. Board of Education* 330 U.S. 1 (1947), pp. 15–16.

[2] *Crisis in Western Education* (New York: Sheed and Ward, 1961), p. 22.

[3] *Church, State and Freedom* (Boston: Beacon Press, 1967), p. 338.

[4] *The First Amendment and the Future of American Democracy* (New York: Basic Books, 1976), p. 70.

[5] Notre Dame, Ind.: University of Notre Dame Press, 1990.

Ronald P. McArthur

THOMISM IN A CATHOLIC COLLEGE

I am very pleased indeed to have been invited to this conference and, further, to have been invited to give one of the papers. I met Chauncey Stillman (and we are here because of his generosity) over twenty years ago, when our good friend Lyman Stebbins introduced me to him here in New York. We became friends, and every year Chauncey sponsored a reception for Thomas Aquinas College at the Yacht Club. We should all remember him in our prayers, for he was indeed a fine Christian gentleman who helped many of us advance the projects for which we asked his help.

The consideration of Thomism in a Catholic college is vast in its implications. The study of St. Thomas is endless. His mind was so great, his heart so fixed on God and the truth, his works so perfect in their thought and expression, that we seem beginners every time we study him. But study him we must if we would form our minds according to the authoritative pronouncements of the Church, and study him we must if we would have any genuine Catholic education. He is not, however, studied much in our time, so perhaps the best way to develop this topic is to reflect first on some of the reasons that prevent us from studying him, and then to give some reasons why we should—even why we must.

There are many reasons given for the neglect of the study of St. Thomas:

1. We do not think his works relevant to the intellectual concerns of the day, which aim so often at the transformation of the world according to our various utopian visions, them-

selves based on philosophical positions antithetical to those of St. Thomas.

2. Most teachers and students in our colleges and universities, including our Catholic institutions, are convinced that truth is not finally attainable, that our whole lives as teachers and learners are taken up at best with the exchange and modification of opinions (not reflecting that one opinion can never be better than another unless something concerning their subject is *known*). While this position is usually hidden behind a multitude of words, it is yet a kind of universal scepticism, finally nihilism.

3. There is virtually no liberal education in our schools. Our students, therefore, cannot as a rule read, write, or think. They are not, as a consequence, prepared to read St. Thomas—or, for that matter, any other great mind. The usual textbooks intend to make the liberal arts unnecessary; one can manage his way through such books without using his mind in any significant way.

4. The mathematical arts are taught, if at all, to very few, and taught very poorly, at that. There is no appreciation, therefore, of ancient geometry, of Descartes' own *Geometry* or of the whole cast of mind of which he was the catalyst. This ignorance of mathematics means that the reader of St. Thomas will not understand much of what he says about the kinds of quantity, about the demonstration proper to mathematics, and about number as quantity and then as it is applied to the nonquantitative. Consequently, large parts of St. Thomas are virtually unintelligible to modern men.

5. It is thought, in almost all academic circles, that the scientific revolution of the seventeenth century (think of Galileo and Newton) has shown that the ancient study of nature, that study most conspicuous in Aristotle, is fundamentally false and misguided. From this it follows that the *Metaphysics* of Aristotle, based as it is upon his works in natural philosophy, is false and misguided as well (think of Hume's ridicule of the *Metaphysics*). It is clear that St. Thomas thought the opposite and

that his theological works are replete with the very notions that supposedly have been shown by the new physics to be false. St. Thomas' own works, therefore, are, as works of human intelligence, fundamentally false and misguided. He is therefore either wholly dismissed or lauded as a brilliant example of medieval thought, itself an unreflective and dogmatic enterprise. (One thinks here of Bertrand Russell, who thought St. Thomas a brilliant thinker whose works were, of course, all wrong-headed.) The consequence of all this is that the Church, which proposes St. Thomas as our master, is herself wrong-headed, and her very teachings irrelevant to any serious education.

6. It is currently thought that theology is a particular and special discipline. The theologian, then, is a specialist, as are the purveyors of other disciplines. Seen this way, theology cannot be a *wisdom*, a discipline that is at once the supreme science and that orders and uses all the others as handmaids in pursuing the truth about God. Since everyone is a specialist and so prides himself, it follows that St. Thomas' whole enterprise is seen as foolhardy if not impossible in our time, especially with the almost exponential growth of more and more specialized disciplines.

7. The reigning doctrine of academic freedom sees all religious belief as a constriction of free inquiry, and those whose thoughts are in any way based upon it are said to have nothing but personal belief, itself deprived of any rational basis. Such religious positions, while conceded to be personally important, are denied the status of communicable knowledge and are hence irrelevant to the intellectual enterprise. Since St. Thomas did indeed believe a religious doctrine, and since those beliefs were indeed a part of his intellectual furniture, he is then discredited as a thinker except for those who might share, personally, his own beliefs.

These are just some of the objections to the study of St. Thomas, but they alone are enough to ensure what we see today—the neglect of the serious study of our greatest theologian and one of the few consummately great minds of all time.

To study St. Thomas, then, the way he should be studied demands that we see our way through the obstacles that prevent us from taking him seriously as our *teacher*, as the one who forms our minds. (I take it that we agree that he should form our minds—that we agree, that is, with the advice and commands of all the Popes since his death that we should study him as our master in the intellectual life.)

Our first task, should we be serious, would be to restore genuine liberal education in our Catholic schools, to help our students acquire those arts that are the ways to wisdom and without which the intellectual life is impossible. This means that our students learn to read and write, acquire the basic disciplines in mathematics, and, in sum, learn to think by acquiring the liberal arts. Such a restoration of liberal education is impossible using textbooks, almost all of them written to escape the difficulties involved in any serious thought. Lectures as the basic mode of teaching must go, for they presuppose, if they are to help the student, that he is already educated enough intelligently to consider what is told him. (Aristotle, if you recall, thought that the generally educated man was not one who was expert in any field but one who could listen to any lecture and judge if that lecture were reasonable or not, if it proceeded from principles proper to its subject, and if it proceeded with fitting arguments.)

The antidote to the lecture is a steady diet of discussion of significant texts, whereby the student attempts first to understand what he can and then to discuss his own understanding with his peers and his teacher. In this way the student can come to have some confidence in the use of his intellect. Let me take the example that is most fruitful in this connection. If one studies Euclid carefully, reflecting on the principles and the propositions, he becomes an incipient mathematician, and with that habit comes a newfound confidence that he can actually see a part of reality truly and that some truths follow from others. This is a first and very important step toward his emancipation from the nihilism that surrounds us and that teaches that there is no such truth about reality. It is a further emancipation from the passive acceptance of everything the professor says, to be regurgitated through examinations.

A study of great works shows, among other things, that the truth, or even a defensible position, has little to do with relevancy. All serious thought, even historical thought, is non-historical; at its best it rises from the constrictions of time and place. No serious student cares much about relevancy, nor does he study primarily to refute the contemporary positions he thinks false. He studies because he wants to know, and he studies contemporary thought insofar as it helps to that end —not because it is contemporary. Hence, St. Thomas' works are not relevant if one means by relevancy whatever occupies the minds of contemporary thinkers. His works are, however, crucial for the intellectual life of the Christian, for they, as do all great works, transcend the shifting ground of fashionable thought and further lead those who wish to know from the right beginnings to the highest and most glorious truths that follow from them.

The serious study of St. Thomas demands, in our time, the serious study of some of the great works of modern mathematics and modern science. I think of Galileo's *Two New Sciences* and Newton's *Principia*, as well as Descartes' *Geometry*, the book that was itself a revolution in mathematics. Descartes shows the power in considering discrete and continuous quantity as one, so that we can come to universal equations applicable to any material object—a method that enabled him to plot algebraically any curve and thus overcome the limitation of Apollonius as he conceives and describes his conic sections. A failure to study Apollonius and then Descartes means that we are incapable of judging what we gain with Descartes, but also what we lose. We are thus rendered incapable, finally, of understanding St. Thomas when he refers to things mathematical, thinking that he means the kind of thing we once encountered in our textbooks, themselves, the more they are advanced, based on Cartesian mathematics as if it were mathematics itself.

An ignorance of Galileo and Newton leaves us ignorant of the power of mathematics in the study of nature, but also ignorant of what such a method leaves out of its considerations. Hence, because of the tremendous success of mathematical physics, both speculatively and practically, it is easy in our ignorance to think that all nonmathematical considerations of nature are now simple-minded and, as Galileo thought, a destructive detour that has impeded our quest to understand the world. Only a study of these important texts in all their grandeur can show that this is not so. One example: Galileo, in solving a problem concerning accelerating motion, says that lines are made up of points, and time of instants (infinitesimals, so small they are immeasurable). This happens to be false, but lest we then condemn Galileo, we can be led to see the importance of such abstractions in his works while understanding what such considerations leave aside. The same is true even more remarkably with Newton. My point is that there is a valid way of considering natural things nonmathematically, and that we all, including physicists, do it either well or badly. St. Thomas, following Aristotle, did it well, and so his metaphysical considerations, again following Aristotle, are valid. They have not been refuted by that scientific revolution that is supposed to have reduced all such thought to the dustbin. Once we are freed from this misconception, we can study St. Thomas without fear that his whole enterprise insofar as it uses natural philosophy is tainted at its roots. (It goes without saying that whenever St. Thomas is wrong, about heavenly bodies, for instance, we follow the evidence available to us—as, by the way, he did when he came to his own positions.) It is not, in other words, a choice between Aristotle's philosophy or modern science, a choice therefore between St. Thomas and modern science.

St. Augustine, in his treatise *On Christian Doctrine*, tells us that the study of nature is important if one is to interpret Scripture well. One sees in St. Thomas the result of a profound concern for the natural order. Augustine and Aquinas are examples that show that sacred theology is not one specialty among many. It is a wisdom, and one of the properties of the wise man is to order—which means that he must see different parts of the intellectual enterprise as constituting a whole in which the inferior parts are ordered to the superior, where the supreme part rules. This means that the theologian at his best sees the order among the various disciplines, sees how they minister to his supreme discipline, and so uses them. If the theologian then is seen as the expert in a special discipline among many, we could never say of him that he was wise, that he saw an order in the intellectual life. Such a position would see St. Thomas' endeavors as almost Quixotic. But such is not the case: anyone who attempts to explain a parable of our Lord is doing the same kind of thing as does St. Thomas; we use other knowledge in our theological considerations either well or badly; there is no choice as to whether we be philosophical.

The position that religious belief is opposed to free inquiry and constricts the intellect in its search for the truth might be so if all religions were false. If, however, there is a true religion, one revealed by God, and a Church that teaches that truth infallibly, then it is of course nonsense to think that one who believes *that* religion is harming his intellect. Our Faith is true, and so belief in it enhances the intelligence rather than harms it and is a great help in the life of intellectual inquiry. There are many examples that come to mind when one reads St. Thomas. We read in the tenth book of Aristotle's *Ethics* that our highest happiness lies in the contemplation of God. As he says, however, this happiness is tainted: because it is difficult to think for a long time, depending as we do on the brain, a material organ; we die and cannot then contemplate God for very long. Our Faith enables us to see the rightness of Aristotle's teaching, and better than we could as nonbelievers. How right Aristotle is, we can see, when we hold that our end is at once beyond anything he thought—seeing God face to face with no cessation of that vision and with no death—but not contradictory to his marvelous insight. St. Thomas, in fact, uses Aristotle to elucidate the teachings of our Faith concerning our final beatitude

—a teaching that at once elevates Aristotle's own thought and enriches our own Faith because of that elevation.

There is another example in Plato's *Statesman*. Plato shows that the rule of law is superior to the rule of man because it is rule by reason. But, he says, because the rule of law is yet through the universal, because justice is applied in the particular, and because there are always exceptions in the application of the universal to the particular, there is something lacking in this rule. There is, then, conceivable another rule, superior to the rule of law. It is the rule of the statesman, the wise man, who, resplendent with virtue, would judge rightly the particular and put everything in its place. Now, however odious this may sound to our democratic ears, we yet believe that there is such a statesman and that he will so judge. Christ our King will come at the end of the world, and he will judge every man in the particularity of all his circumstances, and perfect justice (tempered, of course, with mercy) will result. How rich then, does Plato's insight look when seen with the eyes of faith!

There are, further, many examples of St. Thomas' developing positions that could have been developed without faith but that were developed because he was trying to work out intellectually something he believed by faith. Because, for example, he believed that the sacraments of the new law cause grace, he thought out more completely than ever before the role and significance of the instrumental cause.

I could go on, but let these few examples get us at least to entertain the view that our Faith is a great aid in our intellectual lives, and that far from hindering us, it makes it possible to lead such lives more completely than ever we could without it. St. Thomas is, as in other areas, our best guide here, for he understood the principles of the various disciplines and the distinction of all natural disciplines from sacred theology. He was able, then, to use his Faith positively in the development of sacred doctrine and negatively as an aid in judging philosophical positions. He is that wonderful example of *fides querens intellectum*, the right stance for any Christian thinker.

Since St. Thomas we have, of course, the whole enterprise we call modern philosophy. We should study it with the same care with which we study St. Thomas himself. While fundamentally false in their central theses, there are modern works that illumine our understanding in many ways and whose errors are most instructive. By understanding the great modern thinkers, we can understand St. Thomas better—especially when we read them and him as our contemporaries and give them the attention they deserve.

I close these brief and random remarks with one last thought. Our unity as believers depends first of all on the unity of belief. If, as so often happens, the educated believe one faith and the uneducated another, we do not have in practice the one true Faith. It is, in fact, as if our sometimes modern homilists have the "real" truth and yet preach a "picture" truth to the faithful who could not understand the heights and depths of the new learning. St. Thomas again is the practical refutation of this situation. Take any good catechism, learn it, and think with it. Then study St. Thomas for a lifetime. You will find that you can return to that catechism with the same faith, the same assent with which you began your intellectual life as a Christian. He, then, joins us more completely in the one true Faith, no matter what our learning. He incorporates us, in other words, and there is no separation, in our way toward God, of the learned from the unlearned, the cultured from the peasant, or the preacher from the congregation. This is why he could preach to crowds of mostly unlettered Christians, who flocked to hear his Lenten sermons in Naples.

The restoration of the serious study of St. Thomas, of reestablishing him as our master, seems, if we look at our human condition as it presents itself at the end of our century, practically impossible. Remember, however, that our Holy Church was founded by our Lord, that his Vicars for hundreds of years have espoused St. Thomas as our master, that God Almighty rules the world, and that tremendous and all-reaching changes have appeared as if by a miracle. A change from our present doldrums to the study of the perennial wisdom as is found principally in St. Thomas is not then absolutely impossible. As such, it is something for which we should devoutly pray, for unless we put our minds and hearts to this task, Catholic education might be something we talk about, but there will assuredly be no such reality to which we can point.

PAUL V. MANKOWSKI, S.J.

THE GRAMMAR OF
CATHOLIC WORSHIP

*For the nuns of St. Scholastica Priory and monks of St. Mary's
Monastery, Petersham, Massachusetts, with gratitude from a dull
but loving pupil.*

I remember being taken, as a child of three years, to the local parish church during the Holy Week Triduum and being
deeply moved in seeing that the crucifix above the altar and
the other prime statues were covered in dark cloth. I recall the
feeling of loss and of a peculiarly somber emptiness that the
veiling provoked: something important, and benevolent, was
gone.

I remember too that, at the same age, I was fascinated by
my father's '49 Nash, interested in what made it go. At one
point I opened a large red can in our garage and sniffed the
fluid inside, and I deduced from the burning in my nostrils
that the power in gasoline was nothing else than this capacity
to sting. The engine under the hood mysteriously extracted
the vital essence, the sting factor, from the fuel, and that made
the car move.

As I grew older I learned how an internal combustion engine
really works, and my earlier imaginings were simply recognized
for what they were—wrong guesses—and discarded.

I also came to learn my catechism in time and found out
the reason for the veiling of the crucifix and statues during
the Triduum. And yet it isn't true to say that later understanding obliterated the work of my childish imagination here. Although my early apprehension of the meaning of the veiling

was "prediscursive", catechetical knowledge only confirmed and deepened what I had already grasped before I had words to express it. There was nothing I needed to let go, nothing I believed that I had to cease believing. When I heard the story of Jesus' crucifixion, death, deposition, and burial, I did not need to be "coached" into the proper emotional responses, for these were already in place long before I understood what I was responding *to*. Much later, when I encountered the work of Hans Urs von Balthasar, who erected an entire theology of Holy Saturday with the empty tabernacle as its keystone, I recognized in his insights a consummation or union of discursive reason, intelligibility, with much deeper promptings that were as old as my oldest memories. The fact of the matter is that the Church taught me about God before I was teachable.

The theme of this conference, "The Mind and Heart of the Church", invites us to deepen our capacity for *sentire cum ecclesia* —an expression that means both "to think with the Church", that is, to take her side in dispute, but also to respond as the Church responds, to love and mourn what the Church loves and mourns, to have as our own the heart of the Church as well as her mind. Our worship of God is, or should be, the preeminent occasion of *sentire cum ecclesia*, when our human faculties are engaged in such a way that intellect, will, and emotion are not at war with each other but make a single, simple gesture of adoration.

The Church's worship is the school of ortho-pathy. I use this pedantry by way of contrast to ortho-doxy, that is, having the right opinions. By "orthopathy" I mean the right responses, even the right receptivity. The liturgy teaches us about God not (primarily) as a catechist does, by coaching us in true propositions, but rather by inviting us to react as the Church reacts to Calvary, to respond as the Church responds to Easter, to be receptive to Isaiah, or to St. Luke, or to the book of the Revelation, the way the Church is receptive to them.

I am not arguing, nor do I believe, that right feelings must precede right doctrine or that the liturgy is a kind of kindergarten for dinning in the former. It does not always work that way. Most of us had a sound doctrinal grasp of the Sixth Commandment, "Thou shalt not commit adultery", long before we possessed the emotional equipment in virtue of which it becomes important. By the same token, perhaps a simple phrase in the Eucharistic Prayer, which we have heard and understood perfectly well for twenty or thirty years, may go off inside us like a forgotten land mine at a time when we least expect it, filling us with a radiance of profound emotional satisfaction. Not all worshippers are taught the same lessons in the same order. A second-grader may be given an orthopathic grasp of the *lavabo*, the priest's ceremonial washing of hands, which eludes the systematic theologian for most of his life, even if the latter is orthodox. Moreover, what St. Gregory the Great said about the monastic Rule of St. Benedict is even truer of the liturgy, that "lambs can wade in it and elephants can swim in it": that is, beginners in the Christian life are never drowned but can participate in the Church's worship with total confidence that the authentic teaching of Christ is the "flooring" beneath the entire enterprise; while the very greatest theologians and mystics can sport in the liturgy, throwing themselves into it entirely, and never touch bottom, never plumb the full depth of the mysteries it contains.

The linchpin of orthopathy is the nature of Christian worship itself. St. Augustine hit the bull's-eye in one of his sermons: *nos colimus Deum*, he said, *et Deus colit nos. Nos colimus Deum*, we worship God; *et Deus colit nos*, God tends us, prunes us, cultivates us, pastures us. The pun centers on the verb *colere*, which means both to worship, to "pay cult", and to act as a shepherd or vine-dresser; the theological insight focuses on the reciprocal nature of these activities. Our worship of God neither proceeds from our initiative nor terminates in our personal gratification. Our desire to praise God is itself his gift; moreover, in worshipping God we are tended by him, much as the fig tree in Luke 13 is trimmed and fertilized and watered so as to bear more fruit: *Deus colit nos*. When we worship with

the Church, we are prepared the way soil is prepared to make
it receptive, so that we can accept what God wants to give us
and yield the right fruit in due season.

In principle, there is no aspect of our experience of worship that does not, or cannot, have some meaning pertinent
to life in Christ. The architecture of our place of worship,
the music that accompanies the liturgy, the shape and color of
priestly vesture, the progress of the eucharistic action, and of
course the words spoken by the celebrant and people can all
contribute to the act of worship. Most elements of worship
are the way they are for a reason; most "do their work" even
when, as in the case of children, the reason is not explicitly
known.

For me, the most useful way to picture the way in which the
elements of the Church's worship work together is in terms
of a grammar. By "grammar" here I mean not a book about
a language but rather the system of interconnecting parts of a
language itself, where a language can be any coherent system
of meaning. For example, we might say that mathematics is a
language with a grammar of its own, or even that chess is a
language with a grammar of its own, the grammar in each case
being the rules by which the significant parts are related to each
other and to the whole. The advantage of treating the liturgy
as this kind of grammar is that it shows the importance of consistency while at the same time it allows for development, for
authentic adaptation and change.

Consider one relatively minor element in the Church's worship, that of genuflection. I would maintain that there is no
logically necessary relation between one's bending of the knee
and acknowledging God's majesty, any more than there is a
logically necessary relationship between the sound "frog" and
one particular family of amphibians. Not only are there many
other gestures that, in other systems of worship, are used to
signify humility in the presence of a god, but the act of knee
bending itself has a univocal meaning in, say, the grammar of
football (when a punt receiver performs it in the end zone),

and this meaning is entirely distinct from the equally univocal meaning of the same gesture made in a Catholic Church.

The point is that we want to ask: How does the *grammar* work? How does the element fit into the system? We find, if we are alert, that genuflection is performed to acknowledge God present in the Blessed Sacrament, and to no other purpose. A half-bow is made before images of our Redeemer, such as a crucifix, but to genuflect to a crucifix is to commit a solecism, to sin against the grammar of worship. It is like confusing the honor one owes one's mother in the flesh with the respect one pays to her photograph on the mantelpiece. When a church-goer on Good Friday genuflects to the empty tabernacle before he slides into his pew, or when the principal celebrant at Mass neglects to genuflect before the newly consecrated species, they both betray that they do not understand the grammar or are contemptuous of it. In contrast, Pope John Paul, after distributing Communion at Mass, invariably genuflects to the Blessed Sacrament after he has handed the ciborium to a deacon. Notice: there is no necessary connection between signifier and signified here, but even a child who observed the Pope genuflect in this circumstance would learn *something* about the Eucharist from that event alone. When the grammar is intact, the Church can speak, even to the simple; when the grammar is violated, the result is nonsense.

To take another example, I believe there is no reason a priori why red should be the color emblematic of martyrdom and of the Holy Spirit, while green should signify ordinary time. Yet, when the celebrant and sacristan take some care to *sentire cum ecclesia* on this point, the slow but powerful rhythm of the liturgical year is made palpable to the congregation and provides real nourishment. When Advent gives way to Christmas, when Lent gives way to Easter, it is signaled not only by a change of texts but also by a quickening of the senses as violet gives way to white. However, when Father decides, by his own lights, that orange is a happier color than white for a feast of the Lord, he may score a *coup de théâtre* on a given Sunday, he may succeed in dazzling his audience, but he has also eroded the system of meaning; he has damaged the intelligibility of worship as a whole. He can use orange only in a Pickwickian sense—that is, in such a way that only *he* can explain *his* intended meaning —and that is not how a language works.

Every priest, upon finishing a public Mass, should ask himself this question: What would a very young child, or a mentally defective adult, have learned about God or his Church from this celebration of the Eucharist? If the priest were attentive to the question, he would, I believe, be forced to acknowledge three things. First, there is virtually no aspect of the action or environment of worship so trivial as to have no potential for teaching, for conveying truth or falsehood. This is true even of the silences at Mass. Second, the capacity to teach truth depends on the consistency of action and environment, on the integrity of the whole, on what I have called the grammar. Third, this consistency cannot be a purely personal endeavor but must be something that the overwhelming majority of celebrants strive for in all their liturgical priestcraft. If I am the only one using a certain grammar, I am the only one speaking the language—which is a roundabout way of saying that I am communicating nothing.

Another benefit of consistency, one the value of which is difficult to exaggerate, is that it is a necessary condition for that spiritual freedom in which worship is possible at all. By restricting himself to the confines of the Mass, the celebrant does not curtail the spiritual freedom of his congregation but protects it. C. S. Lewis has explained the paradox in terms such as these: During Mass I can exercise either a critical or a devotional faculty, and the two are mutually exclusive. As my critical faculty is usually alert, it interferes with worshipping God and has to be "lulled to sleep", as it were. The eucharistic liturgy, when enacted properly, is precisely the instrument by which this faculty can be quieted and the devotional faculty engaged. However, this is dependent upon the expectation of participation in the *Church*'s liturgy, not Fr. So-and-so's adaptation of it. For if I have reason to believe that the celebrant will depart from the text or the rubrics, my critical faculty is "on line" whether I want it to be or not. For of course the celebrant's departures may be tendentious or heretical or imbecile or all three. And even if a given celebrant *is* in the end adjudged to have stayed within bounds, I still would have been forced, against my will, to engage in an activity of criticism rather than of worship. I will have been cheated of a Mass.

I admit that very little of what has been said so far gives much help to the worshipper in the pew. In spite of the call of the Second Vatican Council for greater participation in the eucharistic action, the fact remains that layfolk are victims of clerical arbitrariness in the matter to worship to an extent unthinkable before the Council. Simply put, one seldom knows what he will be obliged to participate *in*. Few of us still have illusions in this regard. We are likely to enter a building that has been built or redecorated as an "unstructured worship space", with carpeting on the floor, semiupholstered furniture, potted plants, and canister lighting. Locating the tabernacle often takes some time, and we may be rewarded by the sight of a coy rosewood box tucked away in an alcove where, in a ballpark, the visitors' bullpen would be. There are no kneelers. The atmosphere is kin to that in a waiting room of a Danish gynecologist, and not without reason.

The celebrant enters, garbed in a poncho of rainbow polyester with appliqués suggestive of various bird or plant life, in the manner of that Third World folk art executed in Scarsdale. Forty minutes of cheery autobiography and mild political exhortation may follow, within which the shrewd listener might be able to pick out the rough outlines of the eucharistic sacrifice.

Most lay Catholics I talk to feel "wrung out" after Mass, largely on account of the exertion required to perform two difficult mental tasks that operate at cross-purposes to each other. One task is that of distracting oneself from annoying irrelevancies: one must make a good willed effort to ignore the pointless innovations in the rubrics, the chatty intros of the readings (or of the people who do the readings), the tendentious alteration of collects or eucharistic prayers, and (unless one is especially blessed) the music. The task contrary to distraction is that of *attending* to the eucharistic action. Anyone who has heard a musician in the contemporary mode perform improvisations on a theme will know what I mean, how one has to *strain* to listen for the elusive and oblique suggestions of melody that peek through the calculated dissonance. Similarly, worshippers have to be alert for those scraps of familiar liturgy out of which something like a Mass can be patched together. Small wonder they are exhausted.

A friend who attends a fairly middle-of-the-road church told me recently, "It would be great if parish liturgy were done as it should be, but the fact is that it's not. And for my own spiritual health I just can't keep going to Mass every time with my dukes up." Point taken. How can we speak of cultivating right receptivity when one is forced to choose between "going with the flow", which means complicity in silliness, or fighting against the current, which excludes receptivity *tout court*? It would seem that the model of the Church's worship as a school of orthopathy is a pipe dream, or at best a favor reserved to the happy few.

Though tempting, this view neglects one vital theological consideration: every Mass that has ever been said, with the barest minimum of validity, is an entirely perfect Mass. It is perfect for two reasons: because the victim that is offered is perfect, and because the priest who performs the sacrifice is perfect. It is Jesus Christ who is both victim and priest, and this means that every Mass is an offering no less effective, no less pleasing to the Father, no less redemptive of us sinners, than the sacrifice made on Calvary, because every Mass *is* the sacrifice of Calvary. This is true when the celebrant is in mortal sin or has lost his Faith. This is true when the rubrics are slovenly, the readings inaudible, the homily purest heresy. This is true when the music affects us as do fingernails dragged slooowly across a chalkboard. This is true when Mass is said in a quonset hut, or on the hood of a jeep, or in the kind of hyperilluminated warehouse in which architect and liturgist have conspired to ensure that no stray thought fly heavenward.

Nos colimus Deum, et Deus colit nos. Even when the first part of this formula is stretched to the breaking point, even when what is offered to God is barely recognizable as the Church's worship, the second part remains true. Sometimes we have to make an act of faith that God does indeed nurture us, does indeed tend to us in our worship. Often the tilling and pruning are painful; *very* often we are inclined to object to God's choice of fertilizer. But it is presumptuous to believe that the Perfect Sacrifice, no matter how depraved the circumstances of its execution, cannot work to our good. At each Mass we pray to the Lord, "Look not on our sins, but on the faith of your Church." Surely it is not too much to believe that God *grants* this petition; that in our worship he sees not the pouting and stubbornness of men but his Bride, the Church, at prayer; that contemplative nuns, and theologians, and giddy schoolgirls, and steelworkers, and "pastoral" musicians, and even awed three-year-olds face to face with an empty tabernacle are formed by this consummate priesthood into a single, acceptable body: without spot, without wrinkle, without apricot Dacron® polyester.

JANET E. SMITH

THE LAYWOMAN
IN THE CHURCH

I

It is one of the most ardently held and relentlessly repeated
dogmas of feminism that women have been oppressed and exploited throughout history. Young women today tend to think
that before the 1960s, women were totally subservient to men,
their lives completely occupied in trivial and humiliating tasks.
They believe it is thanks to feminism that women have finally
escaped the ghetto of the home and found that they need not
have as their highest aspiration being Mrs. Cleaver, wife of
Ward, mother of Beaver and Wally.

The myth of the historical subjugation of women has been
dominant in American culture since the midportion of last century. A female historian at the turn of this century, in speaking
of winning the vote for women, stated:

> The true objection to woman suffrage lies far deeper than any
> argument. Giving women the ballot is the visible sign and sym-
> bol of a stupendous social revolution and before it we are afraid.
> Women are one-half of the world but until a century ago the
> world of music and painting and sculpture and literature and
> scholarship and science was a man's world. The world of trades
> and professions and of work of all kinds was a man's world.
> Women lived a twilight life, a half-life apart, and looked out
> and saw men as shadows walking. It was a man's world. The
> laws were man's laws, the government a man's government, the
> country a man's country.[1]

Mary Beard, an American historian, wrote a book in 1946 entitled *Women as Force in History* wherein she attempted to debunk this myth of universal female subjection. Beard labored both to unearth the origin of this myth and to put it to rest. She traces how from about the time of the famous feminist gathering in Seneca Falls, New York, in 1848, the view that women have made negligible contributions to history became the dominant view, one considered incontestable. She attributes much of the blame to the use made of the commentaries on English law written by Sir William Blackstone, who misrepresented English law by reporting that when women married they completely lost their identity in that of their husbands and had no rights of their own. Beard argues that women had many rights in common law, rights not mentioned by Blackstone. Beard substantiates how feminists took Blackstone's misrepresentation of English law as representative of all law and even of the condition of all women, everywhere, at all times.

Beard grants that most histories make little mention of women and their contributions. She thinks feminists are to some extent responsible for this neglect, since she maintains that they are the source of the elevation into gospel truth of the misbegotten notion that women have been no kind of force in history. She claims that this falsehood has blinded historians to the achievements of women. Why should they look for what they will not find, an active role of women in history? She notes, for instance, that in history text after history text, and in encyclopedia entry after encyclopedia entry, no mention is made that in the Middle Ages women as well as men were members of guilds, the chief locus of economic activity at that time.[2] Yet she reports that although there is substantial evidence that such was the case, it is evidence that is suppressed or ignored, since it does not fit the picture feminists and their sympathizers wish to paint.

Indeed, feminists have caught themselves in this trap. Beard notes how in the early decades of the last century, as this feminist myth was being concocted, articles, pamphlets, and books written by women about the achievements of women were abundant.[3] She cites the observation of De Tocqueville, who evidently had eyes to see what feminists were blinded to, that "if I were asked now that I am drawing to the close of this work, in which I have spoken of so many important things done by Americans, to what the singular prosperity and growing strength of that people ought mainly to be attributed, I should reply, 'To the superiority of their women'".[4] Beard observes that in the multivolume work *History of Women's Suffrage*, written in part by Susan B. Anthony, Elizabeth Cady Stanton, and Ida Usted Harper, the very authors of the myth of the historical subjugation of women, chapter after chapter sings the achievements of women throughout the ages both as leaders and as members of nearly every profession.

Beard also reveals what is discovered when historians reject the myth of women's lack of influence on history. She reviews Henry Adams' work *Mont-Saint-Michel* about the twelfth and thirteenth centuries. Adams had become convinced that the energy of women was pivotal to explaining the course of history. He found this amply demonstrated in the period about which he was writing. He argued that men and women experienced more equality in that period than they did in turn-of-the-century America. He also placed enormous emphasis on the pervasive devotion people of that time had for the Virgin Mary. As Beard states, "In the popular devotion to Mary was asserted a passionate attachment to the feminine qualities so directive in the long history of the human race."[5]

Beard marshals impressive evidence to support her contention that many women had access to the best in education during periods of history that historians have largely portrayed as dark ages for women. It is no surprise that in her review of the many women who have made great contributions to history, Beard includes the names of several saints, such as Juliana of Norwich, Catherine of Siena, Catherine of Genoa, and Bridget of Sweden.[6] This list could, of course, grow very long and would not be complete without St. Monica, Clare of Assisi,

Joan of Arc, Margaret of Scotland, Rose of Lima, Zita of Italy, Elizabeth of Hungary, Hedwig of Poland, and many others. On this list, both married and single laywomen feature prominently because of the distinguished services they performed for society.

I am no student of history, but I have long been mystified by feminist claims that women have always been dominated by men and kept in their shadow. I am a classicist by training, and my familiarity with Penelope, Antigone, Clytemnestra, and Medea has made me wary of claims that women were nonentities in Greek society. Literature of every age features women who led full and productive lives, who were perfectly capable of living independently of men, who were great leaders, who could outsmart any man or group of men when necessary. Think of the Wife of Bath, or Lady Macbeth, or Willa Cather's heroines. One assumes that such women were not entirely the figments of the imagination of the writers of epics, drama, and novels. Literature has also featured women who had enviable relationships with men, relationships built upon the self-sacrificing love of both parties; this was certainly true of several of the married saints, but it is also true that some of the female saints consecrated to a life of celibacy were closest of friends with male saints of their times. Those who claim that women played no role in history seem to ignore the evidence of literature, the stories of the women of the Old Testament and New, the saints of old, and the Queens of history.

Indeed, there are some signs that feminists are discovering that women have made contributions to history and that these contributions have not gone altogether unrecorded in Scripture and history texts. Their interpretation of Scripture vacillates between finding it to be the record of the cruel mistreatment of women, such as Jephthah's sacrifice of his daughter, to being a record of the deeds of some truly extraordinary women, such as Ruth, Esther, and Judith, who had books of the Bible named after them.[7] As I will elaborate more below, when we know what to look for, we begin to find that the work of women has been indispensable and truly important but often in hidden and subtle ways.

But it is not only Scripture, literature, and history that should make us resistant to the suggestion that women have made no contribution to history. All around us, in public and private life, we find strong women, women who are as capable as any man, women who would know how to make their mark no matter what the social or economic situation in which they found themselves. The mothers and grandmothers of these women were surely of the same breed; it is an insult to their memory to think that they lived in complete and abject submission to men and never actualized any of their native talents. My own grandmother was a peasant immigrant from Yugoslavia with only two years of education; she worked in a factory, eventually purchased her own home, and raised children, both male and female, who went on to get advanced degrees. She was not a product of feminism; she managed to make her own significant contribution.

To say that women have made substantial contributions to society and history is not, of course, to say that women have always or even often been given their full due and have had the access they should have had to professions and power. This is, after all, a fallen world, and it not surprising that one form that sin most readily takes is in the domination of the weaker by the stronger. John Paul II in his apostolic exhortation on the laity observed that women are the prime victims of a mentality that tends to view people as things to be used and exploited for selfish purposes.[8] I intend to paint no rosy picture that women have always had full opportunity to actualize their talents; this is manifestly and often painfully false. But to say that women at all times were downtrodden and that men had an easy and pampered life wherein they treated women as dirt—with no resistance from the women—is simply a complete misrepresentation of the past. Most people in most times and places have had to struggle to survive, let alone to have the opportunity and leisure to become all that they could be. Many women

have been subject to terribly unjust laws and practices of society but they have not had a corner on the misery that this
world doles out.

II

This prelude about women in history has been advanced to help
me make the same point about women in the Church. We now
labor under the false view that until the present age, women
have not been allowed to make a contribution to the Church.
But women do not "need permission" to make a contribution.
Women are perfectly capable of seeing what needs to be done
and doing it, no matter what resistance they find from society
and the institutional Church. I have mentioned the names of
some of the distinguished saints of the past. But we need not
look to the past; in our own time, we have seen women take
the lead in so many efforts of the right-to-life movement, in
providing care for women with problem pregnancies, in set-
tling refugees, in monitoring and opposing where necessary
the sex education in the public and parochial schools. (This
is, of course, a short list.) Many laywomen have found their
local church or diocese unwilling to assist in these endeavors
and have initiated efforts of their own to see that what must
get done gets done.

I am slowly working my way to my main point. Let me pause
to state that I fear lest the emphasis I have put on history may
serve to skew the picture I am attempting to paint. I do not
think it of the utmost importance that women make a mark
on history or that they receive recognition for it. I think there
are several reasons why the contributions of women receive
little mention in history texts. It is not embittered feminism
to observe that one reason may well be that most writers of
history have been male, and, due to the male ego and male
oblivion, males can be slow to recognize the achievements of
women. This is not the same as to convict males, as feminists

do, of having devised some malicious conspiracy to exclude women from the annals of history, a conspiracy nourished and bolstered by an androcentric and patriarchal culture. After all, Beard found both male and female writers of history guilty of underplaying the female contribution and credited Henry Adams with writing most worthily about the female role in history.

Furthermore, and perhaps more importantly, history being what it is, largely a record of war and politics, it is not surprising that the deeds of men are disproportionately represented in history; war and politics have been the spheres in which there generally has been more male than female involvement. Again, although I believe women have, can, and will make great contributions to public life, I suspect and even hope that this will not become their primary sphere of influence. My primary point is not to insist that women be given their due in history texts. Rather, I believe it is one of the graces and great strengths of being female that females are generally content with making their contributions in hidden ways, in private ways, as well as in public ways. We need not look to pious examples to make the case, but it seems right to note that Mary, Mother of Jesus, is our best example; in many ways she lead an unremarkable life, but her *Fiat* led to her Magnificat; the Almighty did great things for her. All women who fulfill their mission on earth share in the glory of Mary, in the fact that all generations call Mary blessed.

The present widely held view that only activity in the public realm "counts" as worthy activity threatens to subvert and not to enhance the kinds of contributions that women, with their natural gifts and talents, can most readily make. Our age is a public age, one that has nearly altogether lost any appreciation for the private. The private world is largely that of the home, but it is more than that. The private world is the world of the intimate relationships without which we cannot live fully human or happy lives; it is the realm where the individual is cherished and the memories that give us a sense of self and connection are most readily built. The public is the place where we more easily play a role and make a more direct contribution, not to individuals but to the common good or to humanity as a whole. Both realms need their heroes and their saints, but the contributions of the private realm, precisely because they are private, simply cannot receive the recognition that public contributions do. Since our society is intoxicated with the need to acknowledge and reward all achievements and believes that there are no achievements where there is no recognition, the private realm is seen as having no value.

Although women tend by nature to value, appreciate, and nourish what is private, many women have been and are being persuaded or seduced into abandoning the private for what is public. Since women have been succumbing to this seduction, our world has been becoming a more hostile place, to the point that babies are now killed in their mothers' wombs at their mothers' bidding. One hopes that this is the nadir of our degradation. If women continue to abandon the private for the public, human gifts will have a more difficult time flourishing. Indeed, the chief contribution that women can make to the public sphere is to attempt to extend as far as possible and as much as appropriate the values of the private into the public. I just read of a business that spent thousands of dollars to learn how to keep workers happy so they would stay on the job. The finding was that the workers who stay on the job are those who feel that they are appreciated as individuals; this is a finding almost any woman intuitively knows and could provide for free.

Women tend to understand the enormous importance of all those acts that make us feel that our individuality is appreciated. Women understand that creating a welcoming home, or a tasty meal, remembering a birthday, listening to someone's troubles, giving a hug, making a homemade gift, and the like are not trivial acts. They understand that these gestures are instances when the love that flows through all creation surfaces, in a very personally directed way, if only for a moment. They know that the cumulative effect of these gestures and, on occasion, of even just one isolated thoughtful gesture is as important to human well-being as more typically male achievements as building a grandiose skyscraper, staging a successful political campaign, or winning a victory over the enemy.

This dimension of the female contribution has been recognized by some feminists. Nicola Slee, a feminist theologian who has begun to look below the surface, made the following observation about Scripture:

> [The] surface domination of male characterization and the anonymity of women in the parables must not be brushed aside too easily. The need for women to experience and express pain at the sign of our invisibility in Scripture must be recognized and affirmed. However, I suggest that it is possible to find beneath the surface invisibility of women a host of images and situations in the parables which are uniquely evocative of women's lives and experiences, and speak deeply to them.[9]

Slee goes on to explain how several parables feature the domestic as a realm where the presence of God can erupt, and thus the "very world of the everyday is irretrievably shattered, irreversibly transformed". She further states, "This provides no easy solution to the conflicts women experience between the domestic and the professional, home and work, family and society, and others, but it does hint that to discover the presence of God within the confines of the mundane and domestic is radically and explosively to transform these realities."[10] Slee has discovered the hiddenness of the domestic and private and realized that this is a natural place for God to work his wonders.

G. K. Chesterton rebukes women for losing sight of the importance of the private. In a marvelous essay entitled "The Modern Surrender of Woman", he laments that women have surrendered to men. Speaking of the modern woman, he states:

> She has seriously and officially owned that the man has been right all along; that the public house (or Parliament) is really more important than the private house; that politics are not (as woman

had always maintained) an excuse for pots of beer, but are a
sacred solemnity to which new female worshippers may kneel;
that the talkative patriots in the tavern are not only admirable
but enviable; that talk is not a waste of time, and therefore (as
a consequence, surely) that taverns are not a waste of money.
All we men had grown used to our wives and mothers, and
grandmothers, and great-aunts all pouring a chorus of contempt
upon our hobbies of sport, drink and party politics. And now
comes Miss Pankhurst, with tears in her eyes, owning that all
the women were wrong and all the men were right; humbly
imploring to be admitted into so much as an outer court, from
which she may catch a glimpse of those masculine merits which
her sisters had so thoughtlessly scorned.[11]

Perhaps Chesterton is guilty of denigrating the public sphere
in order to make his point about the private sphere, but his
is a playful chastisement of women for abandoning their characteristic wisdom that the private sphere is as important as or
more important than the public sphere.

If women still allowed this basic truth to govern their lives,
there would not be the widespread clamoring for ordination of
women to the priesthood that there is. If women truly simply
wanted to serve and to do so in a humble Christian fashion,
there would be no necessity for them to be priests. Yes, some
women are fighting for the right to be priests because they
believe that the exclusion of women from the priesthood is a
denigration of the abilities and intellect of women. But few of
these have been careful to seek to acquire a true understanding
of the reasons for the Church's restriction of the priesthood to
males. Many simply assume that any instance where men are
permitted to perform a function denied to women results from
a view that women are inferior. The Church has gone to great
lengths to explain that such is not a governing assumption in
the reservation of the priesthood to males only, but few feminists give much evidence of being familiar with the reasoning
of the Church on this matter.

Another insidious modern myth is that for women to be fully

integrated into the Church, women must hold high offices in the Church. Many cite the increasing number of women employed in diocesan offices as a sign of greater sensitivity to the needs of women. I cannot fully enter into this enthusiasm. I am dubious of claims that those in the highest and most visible offices are those doing the most important work. Many teachers do much more good than their principals, many nurses do much more good than hospital administrators, many CCD teachers do much more good than diocesan directors of religious education. Good can be done on high levels, of course, but those who wish to serve and do good should not succumb to the temptation to think that the higher visibility jobs are necessarily those by which the most good is done.

Moreover, many seem to think that now that women are holding such positions, the woman's point of view is being represented, is now being heard. Unfortunately, this view is woefully erroneous. Donna Steichen's book *Ungodly Rage*[12] documents the infestation of Church offices by women who have been greatly influenced by New Age principles and, indeed have participated in witchcraft ceremonies and who generally are hostile to the Church and her teachings. They want to form a new Church from within. Those women who love the Church for what she is and who seek only to form their lives by her teachings often find it very hard to get their concerns heard by the diocesan apparat.

All Christians, both male and female, must accept that it is not performing the sacraments or being employed at a high salary in a diocesan office that is essential to advancement in the Christian life. What is essential to advancement in the Christian life is receiving the sacraments and allowing them to permeate one's life, whatever may be one's calling in life. There is no other key to what the Catholic laywoman—or layman—should be doing. First and foremost she should be deepening her prayer life and her attachment to the sacraments and to understanding the teachings of the Church. As the individual laywoman does that, what she should do next, how she should serve will become clear to her. For there is no one set or type of activity in which the laywoman should serve. Each laywoman is a unique individual in a unique time and place who, as Cardinal Newman says, has a special mission entrusted to her that no other can do.

Granted that each of us has a unique mission, some generalizations can still be made. One task of particular importance the laywoman has is that of attending to the relationships that she has been given and formed. This is the "private" sphere of which I have been speaking. Since most laywomen marry, the relationships they most immediately will be attending to will be those with their husbands and children. However, all women have important relationships to attend to, with members of their family of origin, friends, neighbors, coworkers, and whatever broken wings cross their paths or whomever they reach out to touch.

Edith Stein speaks of women's souls as having as their deepest yearning the desire to love and to be loved. She says a woman's whole being is ordained to this, whereas men in their being are more directed to action and dominating the face of the earth. Clearly, woman's primary vocation as mother is the source and most proper symbol of a woman's natural tendency to be a caretaker, to be compassionate and attuned to the needs of others. For most women, again, the chief arena for exercising this vocation will be in the family. The encyclical *Familiaris consortio* provides a tremendous blueprint for what is entailed in the vocations of those called to family life. It speaks of the "domestic" church, which is the home, the first place of evangelization; it is not only a "saved" community but also a "saving" community.[13] Those who are called to family life can serve the institutional Church best by performing well the work of the domestic church.

The view of women as self-sacrificing nurturers and caretakers is one that generally offends the sensibilities of feminists. Feminists tend to think there are two kinds of women: enlightened feminists and doormats. Feminists promote rugged individualism and think that true adulthood for women means being able to stand alone and be dependent on no man. They believe that the doormats think it right and proper that women be totally subservient to men, that women are to serve men, to confine themselves to taking care of children and keeping house. These doormats, reportedly, think no woman should venture into the public realm and should be satisfied to be a mere nothing so that her husband and children can become somethings. When the "doormats" protest that they have no objection to women pursuing careers, that they consider themselves equal to men, that they, too, think there has been and is much unjust discrimination against women, and that they believe women to have made and to be making remarkable contributions to the human endeavor, these claims do not register with feminists. For when feminists hear motherhood spoken of favorably as a full-time occupation or hear rejections of abortion, contraception, and divorce as necessary to the feminist cause, they discount all else that may be said.

Those of us who have the occasion to give talks critical of some of the items foremost on the feminist agenda are regularly accused of wanting all women to be barefoot, pregnant, and in the kitchen. For feminists, this is the ultimate symbol of oppression, nearly akin to a black man in fetters being dragged off to slavery. Now, my mother spent a fair portion of her life barefoot, pregnant, and in the kitchen, and they were some of the happiest years of her life. She was pregnant not by some man who forced himself upon her but by her husband, whom she loved; she was in the kitchen not as in a prison cell, but in the spot from which she worked wonders in performing acts of love for her family; and her barefootness symbolized for her a lack of restrictions, the freedom to go her own way.

It often seems that many feminists have had an unhappy experience of family life and of men and are tempted to think that their experience is the norm; they find the home oppressive and the workplace liberating and, one suspects, more welcoming than the home. Their experience should not be held up as the norm. The fact is that many women who have had happy experiences of both home and the workplace find the home an environment that places greater demands on them and provides them with greater opportunities for growth. Before giving themselves over full-time to being a wife and mother, many found the workplace challenging, stimulating, and rewarding. But once they become "at home" in the home, they find it no less demanding and rewarding. They find that learning how to live with and please their husbands; learning how to keep a well-organized household; learning how to raise well-disciplined, mannerly, and confident children; and learning how to integrate a prayer life with all their other responsibilities require their full attention and an earnest attempt to acquire many virtues. At the same time, of course, to do their job well they must be anything but doormats. They must learn to see that their own needs are met as well as the needs of those around them. This often requires much delicate and diplomatic negotiation with one's spouse and children.

If Edith Stein is correct (and I think she is) that men are more outwardly directed, it follows that they can easily lose themselves in their work to the neglect of the home. Women, then, must help men take their full responsibility for the home. In the apostolic exhortation on the laity, *Christifideles laici*, John Paul II says so much when he speaks of tasks primarily entrusted to women. The first he mentions is the task "of bringing full dignity to the conjugal life and to marriage". In explaining this, he speaks of how women with "intelligent, loving, and decisive intervention" must help their husbands overcome "forms of absenteeism" to assume their proper roles as husband and father.

Women, of course, have a tendency toward a set of failings that are distortions of their natural virtues; they can tend to timidity, to severe subjectivity, to an excessive love of luxury, and to emotionality, for instance. When appropriate, they must learn to take direction humbly from their husbands. They must, in short, allow their husbands to "husband", to be one who nurtures and cultivates them. Edith Stein speaks of the husband helping his wife develop her talents and, if need be, assisting her to grow in such virtues as courage and self-confidence.[14]

This is not to say that spouses do and ought to undertake marriage as an exercise in improving another, but when necessary, they must gently and truly help each other become better. Certainly marriage is an occasion for two individuals to get to know each other so well that they can truly love, support, and delight in each other, but this does not make it an arrangement for two individuals to pamper and indulge one another. This is not what "total self-giving" means. Our fantasies to the contrary, none of us thrive by having someone attend to our every need, to having life made easy for us. Marriage is a Christian vocation; it is a particular mode of living out the call to holiness and to service. Few marriages can survive unless both parties put away many of their bad ways and are willing to acquire new habits and skills that will enhance the relationship and the working of the household.

Most laywomen will make their most significant contribution to the Church in their formation of a deeply and profoundly Christian household. The home they make must be pleasant and within their means; as Christians they will possess a set of priorities that allow them to escape the materialism of our age. This in itself is a major achievement and an important witness. For instance, those households without televisions tend to be a magnet for creative and social activity; thereby, they spread their good influence widely. It is through the family that most will learn to pray, to receive the sacraments, to respect the teachings of the Church. For mothers with young children, simply learning how to be mothers and how to run a household will be a full-time occupation. As their children grow older and their parenting skills increase, they will naturally find themselves enlarging the sphere of their Christian apostolate; *Familiaris consortio* speaks of the "social role" of the family. For instance, for some this will mean engaging in volunteer activities in the community or parish; others who have

come to love children—not only their own—and who have
learned how to be good parents might open their homes to the
care of foster children or might adopt needy children. Again,
this work will not have high visibility, will not receive mention
in history books, and will not bring one fame and fortune. Yet
this is the work of the Church, the domestic church, and it
will advance the coming of the kingdom.

Not all women, of course, will be wives and mothers, and
many wives and mothers will find themselves at some point in
their lives pursuing careers. What should be the contribution
to the Church of the laywoman who is a professional? Again,
the first and foremost contribution of these women will be
being Christian witnesses in the workplace, doing their job
well there, bringing Christian values to the workplace, allowing their femininity to influence the workplace. As *Familiaris
consortio* states:

> [The equality of men and women] does not mean for women
> a renunciation of their femininity or an imitation of the male
> role, but the fullness of true feminine humanity which should
> be expressed in their activity, whether in the family or outside
> of it, without disregarding the difference of customs and cultures
> in this sphere.[15]

Women must bring the feminine qualities of warmth and compassion to whatever they do. One would expect to find women
gravitating to professions that are person oriented. But even
those drawn to such fields as engineering will find that if they
retain their femininity, the ethos of the workplace will change
for the better sometimes in quite inexplicable ways. If nothing
else, the men will most likely become more gentlemanly in the
presence of truly feminine women. Women in the workplace
might be expected to be especially concerned to see that safety
precautions are observed and that all are treated fairly. Female
legislators, for instance, ought to work to enact legislation to
strengthen the family and protect the helpless, such as the un-
born.

The changes that should be brought about in the workplace by the feminine presence seem to correspond to the second task that *Christifideles laici* entrusts to women, that of "assuring the moral dimension of culture, the dimension—namely of a culture worthy of the person—of an individual yet social life".[16] The Pope goes on to say that "God entrusted the human being to the woman".[17] He elaborates that women have a special sensitivity to the needs of the individual and ought to bring that sensitivity with them to their involvements in public life.

Women with professional skills may be able to put these skills to use in assisting the institutional Church. Parishes need financial advisors and lawyers and educators; women in these fields may consider volunteering their professional expertise. They may be in an especially good position to assist organizations who serve the marginalized in society. Nor should stay-at-home mothers and professional women consider each other adversaries. Each can easily think the other has abundant time to do various volunteer work and put unreasonable demands on each other. As Christians, they should recognize that both avenues of life can be directed toward serving the Lord, just as both can be directed to selfish purposes; they should seek to fulfill their own vocation well and not diminish the achievements of the other, or envy them either.

Finally, we must close on a note that none of us are really called to "do" so much as to "be". American society is still obsessed with the work ethic, with the notion that only a day where much is done is a good day. This attitude, again, keeps us from simply "being", from being with and for one another. It keeps us wedded to the public arena; we measure ourselves by how big our salary or car or house is, or by how often we get our names in the newspaper. The story of Martha and Mary will always be to the point; the better part is the part of being attentive to the good that is before us. We must come to relish the private; we must "be", and largely be contemplatives who will sit and marvel at God's goodness and listen to his love. Women will see God's goodness easily and often in other human beings and should thus attend to them as God's beloved creations. We must, as Mary did, treasure all things in our hearts, for it is really what happens in our hearts and through our hearts that is of utmost importance. A woman best serves the Church by seeking holiness; she must then abandon herself to whatever God directs her to do as a part of that quest. We must not limit him in our lives but must accept whatever he intends at each stage and each moment, however ordinary or unconventional his call is.

NOTES

[1] Mary R. Beard, *Woman as Force in History: A Study in Traditions and Realities* (New York: Macmillan, 1946), citing M. Carey Thomas, p. 21.

[2] Some more modern historians have begun to redress this neglect of women's importance in history. A correction has been made, for instance, on this matter of female participation in guilds. See, for instance, Barbara Tuchman, *A Distant Mirror* (New York: Knopf, 1978), pp. 216ff.

[3] Beard, p. 74.

[4] Ibid., p. 74-5.

[5] Ibid., p. 206.

[6] Ibid., p. 265.

[7] For interesting and often credible readings of the role of women in Scripture, see Ann Loades, ed., *Feminist Theology: A Reader* (Louisville, Ky.: John Knox Press, 1990).

[8] John Paul II, *Christifideles laici, The Lay Members of Christ's Faithful People* (Boston: Daughters of St. Paul, 1988).

[9] Nicola Slee, "Parables and Women's Experience", in Loades, p. 41.

[10] Ibid., p. 42.

[11] G. K. Chesterton, *What's Wrong with the World, Collected Works of G. K. Chesterton*, vol. 4 (San Francisco: Ignatius Press, 1987).

[12] Donna Steichen, *Ungodly Rage: The Hidden Face of Catholic Feminism* (San Francisco: Ignatius Press, 1991).

[13] John Paul II, *Familiaris consortio* (Boston: St. Paul Editions, 1981).

[14] Edith Stein, *Essays on Women*, Collected Works, vol. 2 (Washington, D.C., Institute of Carmelite Studies, 1987), p. 76.

[15] *Familiaris consortio*, sec. 23, p. 41.

[16] *Christifideles laici*, p. 133.

[17] Ibid., p. 134.

ALICE VON HILDEBRAND

CHRISTIANITY AND
THE MYSTERY OF SUFFERING

Introductory Reflections

In his great novel *The Brothers Karamazov*, Dostoyevsky states
that the earth is soaked from its crust to its center with the
tears of humanity.[1] This fearful statement reflects a fact that
only shallow optimism can deny. This earth is a vale of tears.
At every hour of the day, all over the world, there are people
who are suffering: be it hunger, be it sickness, be it bereave-
ment, be it injustice, be it brutality, be it lonesomeness, be it
lack of love, be it despair. And suffering humanity raises the
question: Why?

That man is made for happiness, that he longs for it with
every fiber of his being, and that he keeps striving for it and
hoping for it cannot be denied. This longing for happiness is
deeply embedded in the human soul. It commands many of
man's motivations and actions, yet happiness seems so elusive
that the most fortunate human beings can only speak of mo-
ments of deep happiness. Who are they who can claim that their
whole life is nothing but a continuous flow of overwhelming
joy?

The greatest thinkers all raise the question: Why must man
suffer? There is not one thinking being who is not tortured
by a reality that, much as he tries, he can neither elude nor
eliminate. Those who believe that happiness can be univer-

sally guaranteed by adhering to some new system of thought have usually been the instruments of greater unhappiness and of more formidable torments.

Often, men raise their fists and accuse God, their Creator, as the one responsible for the tears that water this earth. The reality of suffering seems to pose one of the most serious obstacles to the belief in God's existence. I know people who deny it for reasons that are so shallow that they do not deserve a refutation. Down-to-earth materialists are likely to reject his existence because they have never seen God under a microscope or through a powerful telescope. Such intellectual shallowness does not merit any notice.

However, when a person, confronting the intensity of real suffering, raises the question in despair; "How can a God who is both infinitely good and infinitely powerful permit such tortures?", we face an insoluble mystery. Faith, however, can shed light upon it.

Our concern is not to address this challenge. We leave this to those whose spirituality and well-grounded theological knowledge equip them to do so. But one thing is certain: it is man's duty to search for the meaning of suffering, for every meaningless suffering, be it only the prick of a needle, is unbearable.

The modest purpose of this lecture is to reflect on the meaning of suffering. Any ray of light shed on this mystery is bound to be a blessing for suffering humanity. On the other hand, the conviction that suffering is meaningless is bound to throw men into a state of revolt and despair.

One thing is certain: suffering is something terrible, something we all dread, something that does violence to our nature. Many people spend their lives trying to calculate how best they can escape from suffering. How many mean, wicked, or even criminal actions have been committed for the sake of evading possible sufferings!

There are people who commit suicide because they can no longer face the intensity of their sufferings. Reading about the lives of people who have been locked up in prisons and concentration camps shows us that the temptation to take one's life is a "classic" temptation when suffering reaches a certain degree of intensity, with no end in sight. In his masterpiece *Le Mie Prigioni*[2], the pious Silvio Pellico relates that this temptation arose more than once during the ten years of his incarceration in various jails.

Our reflections here will be placed in a Christian framework. The Bible makes it plain that suffering came into the world as a punishment for the sin committed by our first parents. Prior to this dreadful moment, Adam and Eve had been placed in an earthly paradise from which they were banished forever as a punishment for their proud disobedience.

Suffering is a necessary consequence of sin. I am far from claiming that this will give us a key to our riddle, but at least it will place it in the right framework and will help us shed some light on this mystery.

But suffering is but one consequence of original sin; these consequences were manifold, and theologians have elaborated on them at length. Let me simply underscore one that is particularly pertinent to our topic. Our intellect has been darkened by sin. Because of this darkening, the intellect is likely to misinterpret the very fact of suffering. The temptation to make God responsible for all our woes is a case in point, for we now tend to put the blame and responsibility for evil on someone else and not on ourselves. Adam put the blame on Eve; Eve told God that she was tempted by the serpent. Now, we, poor, nearsighted creatures, often choose to blame our Creator!

Obviously sin is inconceivable in creatures that are deprived of intellect and will. The very fact that man has been given ontological freedom, that is, the capacity to make decisions for which he bears the full responsibility, enables him to make morally wrong and evil decisions, and this is what constitutes sin.

In granting man freedom, God has taken a tremendous risk —the risk that this human creature would abuse this gift. This, alas, is what took place when Adam and Eve disobeyed God and tried to become gods without God.

Plato is remarkable among the ancient philosophers in that he clearly rejects the grave error of making God responsible for evil. He writes: "We must fight to the last against any member of the cities of the Republic being suffered to speak of the Divine, which is good, as being responsible for evil."[3]

Plato's stand proves that even though man's intellect has been darkened by sin, nevertheless, this same intellect, as long as it remains reverent and truth-seeking, is capable of perceiving how false it is to escape from moral responsibility by putting the blame on God.

But the danger remains, and, alas, too many turn against God with defiance and make him responsible for evil.

Throughout the centuries, great minds have addressed themselves to the question we are now raising, and many of them have contributed deep and illuminating thoughts on the subject. Nevertheless, the reality of evil and suffering remains a mystery.

Gabriel Marcel, to his credit, makes a distinction between what he calls "problem" and what he calls "mystery".[4] Basically, a problem is an objective difficulty, outside of myself, that can be solved, and eventually will be solved. A mystery—and Marcel limits his discussion here to natural mysteries—is an enigma closely related to myself, and even though light can be shed on it, the dimension of mystery will always remain.

It is a classic human temptation to try to treat a mystery as a problem and to force a solution on something that can never be completely clarified on this earth.

A case in point is Marxism. It is Marx' claim that suffering is caused by economic, social, and political injustice. Some grab too much of the earth's resources, to the detriment of others, the proletariat. This unfair unbalance can be corrected by making the all-powerful state the sole possessor of money and property. The state will then distribute wealth equitably and open the door to an earthly paradise.

We need not elaborate on this view. History has effectively shown that Marxism leads to gulags—another word for earthly hells.

Buddhism too offers a solution to the "problem" of suffering, a solution that is much superior to the Marxistic one because it is more spiritual. But it is also fraught with dangers. Like the latter, it challenges one to a radical change of perspective —not in the sphere of economics but in one's attitude toward existence.

The Buddha promises the elimination of suffering to those who, following his doctrine, adopt the right attitude toward human life and give the right response to what this life truly is. Suffering need not be. It is a consequence of a wrong way of interpreting facts; by correcting this distortion, one is guaranteed liberation from this evil.

The Buddha was born a prince. Anxious to protect their son from the woes of human existence, his parents placed him in a palace, where he was shielded from whatever was depressing or sad. But one day the young man managed to leave the palace's enclosure and, within a short span of time, made the acquaintance of poverty, sickness, and death. These experiences shook him to the very depth of his being and revealed to him in a flash what was to become the very core of his doctrine: namely, that human existence is to be equated with suffering. Consequently, suffering is ineluctable as long as man allows himself to be enslaved by a craving for existence. It is by a radical transformation of one's outlook on the meaning and nature of life that one is offered a promise of salvation and liberation from the chains of suffering.

This is to be achieved by stifling within oneself this innate craving for existence, for all emotions that trigger pain are to be traced back to it. The Sakyamuni achieved this feat by a radical desubstantiation and depersonalization of whatever we experience. In other words, man's spontaneous interpretation of reality is totally distorted. He must correct his intellectual vision and understand that the world—as he sees it—is an illusion. He who obediently follows the technique taught by the Buddha is promised liberation and will enter Nirvana.

How different from the Judeo-Christian teaching that after creating the world God saw "that it was very good".[5] How far removed from the Gloria of the Mass resounding with the joy that "heaven and earth are full of God's glory"! To the Christian, the world is good, but, because of sin, it has become a "vale of tears". To the Buddhist, existence is negative and must therefore be transcended. To the Christian, life is a tremendous gift, and even though it implies suffering, this suffering has a deep meaning that transfigures it.

That Buddhism always has had and still has an enormous appeal cannot be denied. Not only does it promise liberation from the fearful reality of suffering, but, moreover, it offers concrete means of achieving this deliverance. It is up to us to enjoy an unruffled calm; it is up to us to become free from the shackles of suffering.

For years, American campuses have been invaded by Oriental literature, inviting students to make the acquaintance of "transcendental meditation" and promising them a happiness that their materialistic outlook on life prevented them from enjoying. There is no doubt that very many of them have turned to the East in the hope of finding a peace that had previously eluded them.

There are various reasons that explain why many young people turn Eastward for a solution to the riddle of human existence and why it did not even occur to them to probe whether the Christian West had anything to offer to quench their spiritual thirst.

First, for years the West has been in the throes of a severe spiritual crisis. A whole generation has been deprived of the benefits of an authentically Christian education. Alas, our youth are spiritually starving, be it because their religion classes have given them stones instead of bread, be it because of the desacralization widespread in our churches. Men cannot live from bread alone. Is it surprising that young people turned to the golden promises offered by the mysterious East? It is there that they hope to find wisdom, sacredness, a sense of mystery from which they have been deprived in the Western world, bogged down in its dazzling scientific accomplishments, coupled with a complete desacralization of human life and a positivistic elimination of the mysteries of human existence, be it love, birth, or death.

Moreover, Buddhism offers us a spirituality stripped of humility, and this is terribly tempting to fallen man. There is no need to recognize one's guilt, to acknowledge oneself to be a sinner, desperately in need of help. All we need do is to discover that our outlook on human existence has been erroneous and to correct this misconception by means of the wise teaching of the Buddha. In other words, man is capable of achieving self-redemption.

There are two things that we human beings fear more than anything else: suffering and humiliation. And these two fearful things are precisely eliminated in Buddhism: one is promised liberation from suffering, and, simultaneously, one does not need to recognize oneself to be a miserable sinner, constantly in need of divine help. On the contrary, one can achieve "self-redemption" by one's own efforts. But let us not forget that the attempt to become gods without God (self-redemption) is original sin.

There is an abyss separating Christianity and Buddhism—something that has been clearly seen by Chesterton. True, in the two "religions" these are striking similarities, but as my late husband often remarked, these are "false" similarities. Let me mention but two of them: both in Buddhism and in Christianity, one can speak of a "metanoia", of a need to correct and change one's vision. But whereas in Buddhism this "metanoia" refers exclusively to the correction of a "cosmic illusion" that makes us believe in the substantiality and the individuality of things, in Christianity this "metanoia" consists of shedding the illusions about ourselves that our pride has nurtured and humbly turning to God for help. The first is an intellectual metanoia; the second is essentially a moral metanoia, based on humility.

Another misleading similarity is to be found in the sentence "love your neighbor as yourself". In the Buddhistic world—a world that is systematically depersonalized and desubstantialized—there is room neither for true love nor for reciprocity. Man having no "self", he can in fact love neither himself nor his neighbor. The famous Buddhistic "compassion" is essentially an ascetic practice that aims at detaching oneself from all things. But in Buddhism—as Father de Lubac, S.J., has remarked—love of neighbor, far from being a response to the lovableness of our neighbor—image of God—is in fact a means of liberation.

In contrast, the very core of Christianity is to be found in the existence of a personal God who is love, a God who has created the world and made man to his image and likeness. Each human being is a unique, irreplaceable person and not a cosmic illusion. Love is the ultimate secret of Christianity, and love of neighbor is a partaking in God's love for another human creature and not a necessary step in the process of radical detachment from cosmic illusions.

The Buddha was a great pedagogue and knew that hatred, envy, revenge, trigger "negative" emotions that deprive one of the calm that is essential to liberation. His pragmatism taught him that he alone can enjoy inner peace who has freed himself from the claws of an illusive reality.

If we compare a statue of the Buddha, with his enigmatic smile, irradiating unruffled calm, and the tortured figure of Christ on the Cross, we are bound to raise the question: How can anyone choose to follow the latter? For on the one hand, we are promised self-redemption and the elimination of suffering; on the other, we are promised humility and the cross. Are Christians masochists, as Simone de Beauvoir claims? Do they have a perverse attraction for suffering and humiliation? If she is wrong, how is one to explain that millions and millions of human beings have chosen to follow Christ to Calvary, to carry their cross, for Christ said, "Let him who wishes to become my disciple, carry his cross and follow me"? In order to answer this question, we ought to realize that there is a "mystery" of suffering on which no light can be shed as long as we view it as a problem to be solved.

The perennial temptation to believe that man can find a key that will enable him to eliminate suffering remains. Again and again, politicians try to sell their ideal of "a new world order" or "a new age" in which justice and peace will reign. But nothing is said about sin. The necessity of purifying oneself first and foremost is usually left very much in the shade, and most do not even perceive any connection between world peace and the elimination of moral evil.

The modest framework of this talk does not allow us to examine in any detail the attitude of the Greeks toward suffering. We shall limit ourselves to saying that the early Greeks saw suffering as an expression of the wrath of the gods; for some reason, they targeted an individual and placed him in a situation that would lead to dreadful sufferings and ultimately bring about his downfall.

A Greek proverb found in Euripides, "*Quos vult Jupiter perdere, dementat prius*"[6] (Jupiter renders insane the person he wants to destroy), illumines this position and is strikingly expressed in some of the great Greek tragedies of the fifth century B.C.

But in Plato, as we saw, we find an intellectual awakening that, by refining its conception of God, refuses to make him responsible for human woes. Plato rightly sees that man is responsible for moral evil, which in its turn inevitably leads to suffering.

The Chosen People established a link between sin and suffering. Throughout the Old Testament we see that unfaithfulness to God leads to punishment and therefore suffering. This sacred book is pervaded throughout by a deep sense of man's need for redemption—a redemption that he cannot achieve unaided.

But it is our claim that Christianity not only gives a unique meaning to suffering but also teaches its disciples the art of suffering. Let us first examine briefly how Christianity teaches men the art of suffering.

1. Elimination of Illegitimate Sufferings

The first step is to eliminate what my late husband used to call "illegitimate suffering", that is, a type of suffering that, painful as it might be, need not be suffered at all, provided the patient adopts the right attitude toward God and toward life. A few examples will shed light on this.

a. Vanity

There are what we might call "self-manufactured" sufferings. In her novel *Pride and Prejudice*, Jane Austen illustrates admirably this type of illegitimate suffering. I am referring to the ludicrous character of Mrs. Bennet, the mother of five girls, who gives vent to her bitter disappointment over the fact that her neighbor has won the contest of matchmaking. Upon finding that this neighbor's oldest daughter just got engaged, she exclaims, "Nobody is on my side, nobody takes part with me. I am cruelly used. . . . Nobody can tell what I suffer! But it is always so, those who do not complain are never pitied. . . . Lady Lucas will have a daughter married before I have."[7] Do I need to add that she needs handkerchief and smelling salts, and that her somewhat cynical husband offers her very little sympathy?

Obviously such an explosion of feelings triggers our laughter, and rightly so. There is no doubt that Mrs. Bennet is close to hysterics, but it is just as clear that there is no objective reason whatever for her antics. That her silly vanity should be wounded by the news is true indeed, but this does not justify the intense, purely subjective suffering that she is undergoing.

If she were not eaten up by vanity, she would not suffer at all. Much as we try, we cannot commiserate with her. All we can achieve is charitably to control our hilarity. She suffers, but she need not suffer at all. The fact that someone gets engaged is a ground for rejoicing, not one for going into hysterics. What Mrs. Bennet is undergoing is triggered by her own fault. It would be simple to eliminate this "suffering" by disavowing her vanity and fighting against her self-centeredness.

Years ago, my late husband and I visited an elderly Spanish aristocrat who told us what she considered to be the most bitter day of her life. She was eighteen and was going to her first ball. She came from a rich family and already had several beautiful pieces of jewelry. She was convinced that she was going to be the queen of the ball. But upon entering the ballroom, she saw one of her acquaintances whose attire and jewels were much more beautiful than hers. All of a sudden, all the joyful anticipating that she had experienced turned to bitterness and gall. The glittering lights dimmed, the music seemed discordant: she was wounded in her vanity. She repeated, "It was the most bitter day of my life."

Obviously this story also brings one to laughter. It seems ridiculous that such an insignificant event can fill a person with rancor. But vanity—another sad fruit of original sin—is so ingrained in fallen man that a lack of recognition of our "merits" can fill our souls with gall. How many authors cannot stand to read the book reviews written about them? How many composers are led to despair by a lack of appreciation of their work? How many intellectuals become sour because their "genius" (real or imaginary) is not properly appreciated? How many women would sell their souls to be called the most beautiful, the most elegant, the most graceful of creatures?

Vanity is a bottomless object of inspiration for the writers of comedies, because it is ridiculous. We all tend to overestimate ourselves and assume that we possess admirable qualities that, in fact, are in no way ours. The discrepancy between what we would like to be and what we are, and how others gauge us, is bound to create a hiatus that is extremely painful. There is a very simple answer: humility. It is incredible how many sufferings are unknown to the humble person who, thanks to God's grace, has overcome his innate narcissism. It is high time that a book be written entitled *Humility, the Key to Mental Sanity*. We are not denying that the person whose vanity has been wounded suffers intensely, but the whole question is: Is this suffering inevitable?

b. Hypersensitivity

There are people who are highly sensitive. In dealing with them, one must always be on the lookout for fear of offending them. They are likely to interpret negatively every word one says. A big problem can develop out of the most innocuous remark.

One cannot change the temperament with which one is born, but one can either freely choose to become the slave of one's temperament or learn to guide it in such a fashion that this sensitivity—which is a gift—is used for love and not put at the service of self-centeredness.

There are plenty of "feelings" (such as moods) that arise in us spontaneously that should not be taken seriously. There are "right" feelings (such as contrition, love, compassion), and these feelings should be sanctioned by our will; and there are wrong feelings (such as envy, anger, revenge), and these feelings should be "disavowed" and rejected by our will.[8]

There is no doubt that hypersensitivity—a disproportionate response to daily events—is a great source of suffering. There are persons who groan from morning to night under the weight of imaginary offenses. But man has been given reason, and he ought to distinguish between real offenses (which should be forgiven) and imaginary ones, which should be "dashed to pieces on the Rock that is Christ".[9]

Great sensitivity is a precious gift, but the meaning of this gift is to be other-centered; its caricature is to be self-centered.

We all prefer sensitive persons to those who seem to have a bovine temperament. Nothing disturbs the latter because they are too thick-skinned to feel anything. But sensitivity is to be purified. This is beautifully exemplified in the life of St. Thérèse of Lisieux. From the time that she was four, when she lost her mother, until she was thirteen, Thérèse was so hypersensitive that she broke into tears for no reason at all. In her autobiography, she calls these nine years "the sorrowful years", even though she was leading a life that, to many of us, would seem ideal, surrounded by a saintly father, to whom she was bound by the most tender affection, surrounded by loving sisters, living in security and peace. Yet in her autobiography she refers to those years as being "sorrowful", whereas from the time she entered the Carmel, where she chose a life of suffering and crucifixion, she enjoyed a deep peace despite the constant trials a Carmelite confronts. Her sensitivity had not decreased; it had been purified. By eliminating illegitimate sufferings, she gained the strength of carrying her daily cross in peace and joy.

Thérèse had prayed for years that God might grant her the grace of putting her sensitivity at his service, and God granted her request after midnight Mass shortly before she turned thirteen.

Hypersensitivity becomes an illegitimate source of suffering when it is self-centered; as we saw, a sensitive heart is given to us to feel for others and to love them more deeply and more tenderly. But since original sin, it tends to degenerate into a maudlin self-centeredness that not only is disastrous but also causes great pain for the sensitive person.

However, thanks to prayer and grace, the Christian is given the means of purifying his sensitivity, so that his heart will resemble more and more the Heart of the God-Man, the Sacred Heart, "*fornax ardens caritatis*".[10]

c. Self-will

One of the keenest sources of suffering, and one that is strikingly illegitimate, is self-will. Being persons, we have received the immense gift of having a free will. But this gift is, alas, often misused. Instead of realizing that it is given to us freely to serve and love our Creator, we are tempted to believe that it entitles us to think of ourselves as having the right of doing whatever we please, because we please.

We all have wishes and desires. Assuming that they are morally legitimate, we are entitled to pursue them. But the legitimacy of our desires does not guarantee that we can reach our goal. Much as we try to attain certain ends, numerous are the factors that are not under our control and contravene our plans. The temptation, then, is likely to arise in us to consider ourselves to be the hapless victims of an unjust fate and to suffer intensely because our will has not succeeded in controlling the flow of human events. Surprising as it may sound, there are people who suffer more intensely from the fact that they have been unable to reach the aim they have set to themselves than from the frustration of their desire. In other words, the opposition to what they want is often worse for them than the loss of the object they want to attain. The "I wanted it" then becomes an absolute. Maybe this aim was not important, but the very fact that a person wanted to attain it and has not succeeded triggers a state of rage that is very painful.

St. Thérèse of Lisieux once again teaches us how to overcome this type of suffering: "I have never wanted anything except what God wanted."[11] By fully conforming her will with God's will, she not only eliminated a source of illegitimate suffering; she also, not having drained her strength through illegitimate suffering, had the spiritual vigor necessary to carry the heavy crosses that God had chosen to place on her way to holiness.

We tend to forget that man is a creature and that his free will was not given to him to become the slave of his arbitrary wishes and desires but to serve God. It is incredible how an obstruction of one's desires can throw a person off balance. We all know people who go into tantrums like badly brought-up children when their wishes are contravened. I am deeply convinced that a large chunk of human suffering is to be traced back to this defeat of our will. But it should be obvious that if man is free to set his mind upon a certain aim, he is also free to let it go and choose not to will it. The fact that a person desperately wanted to take a trip and that this was not granted to him offers him the opportunity of renouncing it freely and in so doing of liberating himself from the "cross" of having his will kept in check. In other words, it is up to the individual to liberate himself from a weight that he himself has placed upon his own shoulders. Alas, since original sin, this stubborn self-will is so deeply ingrained in us that Kierkegaard does not hesitate to say that even though we may love another person ardently, we still are tempted to love our own will more than the beloved.[12] The saints are those whose will fully conforms to God's will; this is why they are "free", and this is why they can carry tremendous burdens with peace and joy—nay, with apparent ease.

d. Self-pity

Another source of illegitimate suffering is self-pity, and yet, it is a trap into which most of us are likely to fall as soon as we are afflicted by great (or even small) evils. The reaction of our fallen nature is to feel incredibly sorry for ourselves, to dwell upon our woes, to magnify them, to keep a ledger of all the sufferings that we have endured since our very youth —and then, crushed by this impressive catalogue of woes, to feel entitled to wallow in self-pity.

The sad thing about self-pity is that it bogs us down into a mire of tragic memories—many of which are amplified by a wild imagination. Finally, we succeed in convincing ourselves that no one—absolutely no one—has ever endured such torments; no one has ever been so unfairly treated. (Jean-Jacques

Rousseau's *Confessions* are most revealing in this respect.) This conviction, in its turn, depletes us of all the strength that God has given us to carry whatever cross has been put on our shoulders. Self-pity is a sort of psychological leak that is bound to lead to the collapse of the person who has fallen into its grips.

Good psychologists would all agree that self-centeredness and self-pity are first cousins, and that the best cure to free oneself from their tentacles is to turn to others, to get interested in their sorrows, to try to heal their wounds. But those who wallow in self-pity, far from showing interest in other persons' problems, often are particularly callous and hard-hearted. Somehow, they feel that anyone's claim to compassion is an offense directed against themselves—they who alone truly deserve to be pitied. They want to prove to themselves and to the world that they alone know suffering, that they alone deserve sympathy; they alone are victims in the full-fledged sense of this term.

But Christianity invites us to contemplate Christ dying on the Cross out of love for us. And this very contemplation will lead us to say with the good thief, "We are receiving the due reward of our deeds; but this man has done nothing wrong."[13]

e. Envy

Envy is one of the ugliest traits affecting man as a fallen creature. The envious person is deeply unhappy over the fact that another person possesses something of which he himself is deprived. In some cases, envy is "remedied" when the envious person manages to be on a par with the object of his envy. Sadly enough, there are many cases in which the envious person is satisfied as soon as the person of whom he is envious is deprived of what he previously possessed. It is a well-known fact that if everybody were poor, poverty would not be considered to be such a terrible evil. This is strikingly formulated in the Italian proverb "*Mal commune, mezzo gaudio*" (a common woe is half a joy).

The envious person suffers tortures; one says that a person is "green" with envy. It is even bound to affect a person's health, because—like a subtle poison—it penetrates into a person's soul, and his soul inevitably will affect his body.

Envy is an ugly trait, but, alas, very widespread. Envy is constantly used as a tool of political propaganda, to whip up the envy of the have-nots toward those who enjoy rich possessions. It is a favored tool of communist propaganda. But once again, this pain, which like a thorn penetrates into our very being, is something that we allow to tear us to pieces. To paraphrase Dietrich von Hildebrand: as free beings, we have the capacity to disavow these illegitimate feelings, to refuse to acknowledge them as our valid position toward others and, in so doing, to "decapitate" them, prevent them from producing their venom, and liberate ourselves from their chains.[14]

f. Pride

This vice is probably the worst source of illegitimate sufferings and often leads to what Kierkegaard so aptly calls the despair of defiance.

Pride is the sin par excellence, and alas, since the fall of our first parents, it is the very stuff of which we are made. It is not our purpose to discuss this vice. Spiritual writers have been eloquent on the subject.[15] All we wish to do is to show that pride, in all its forms, causes unbearable sufferings in the proud man and can actually lead him to despair.

I shall limit myself to brief remarks concerning the difficulty that a proud man has of saying the words "thank you" and "forgive me". These words rank among the most important in the human vocabulary, and yet the proud man detests them. For "thank you' implies a recognition that we are indebted to another person. In thanking him, we acknowledge that we are his debtor and therefore in an inferior position toward him; this is something insufferable to the proud man. He wants to be in command; he wants to be in the superior position; he does not want to owe anything to anyone. Alas, I know people who refuse to taste the sweetness of the words "thank you", which embody our gratitude toward those from whose goodness we have benefited.

Proud people live in a constant state of cramp and tension. They—like all of us—often need other persons' help, but it is fascinating to watch the detours that they invent in order to get help without undergoing the humiliation of asking for it.

The words "thank you" are so precious because they express perfectly man's metaphysical situation. For, as St. Paul wrote: "What have you that you did not receive?"[16] and the same apostle admonishes us to "abound in thanksgiving".[17] The proud, ungrateful heart is always unhappy, for there is an indissoluble bond between gratitude and happiness; nay, gratitude is a key to happiness.

The agonies experienced by a proud man have been strikingly formulated by Kierkegaard, who, describing the satanically proud man, writes:

> Even if at this point God in heaven and all his angels were to offer to help him out of it—no, now he does not want it, now it is too late, he once would have given everything to be rid of this torment but was made to wait, now that's all past, now he would rather rage against everything, he the one man in the whole of existence who is the most unjustly treated, to whom it is especially important to have his torment at hand, important that no one should take it from him—for thus he can convince himself that he is in the right.[17]

The devilishly proud man not only is incapable of saying "thank you", but he is still more incapable of saying "forgive me". For to ask for forgiveness is to recognize that we have sinned toward God and offended other human beings. In saying "forgive me", we therefore acknowledge our sinfulness and our guilt. This is something that to a proud man is unbearable. That he suffers incredibly cannot be denied. What he is going through is truly demonic. But why put up with this crushing suffering when it is self-inflicted? In order to change his course, the proud man would need help—God's help—and this is precisely that for which he refuses to beg. In some perverse fashion, he prefers, as Kierkegaard has shown, the tortures of hell to calling for assistance, and he truly suffers hell. For hell is hatred, ingratitude, resentment, and there is no doubt that many people already taste hell on this earth.

Once again Christianity offers us the answer: it is by contemplating the God-Man, he who took the form of a slave[19] and endorsed our humanity so that we could partake of his Divinity,[20] that the wounds caused by our pride may be healed and that we may learn to rejoice in being nothing, so that he can be everything in us.

2. The Meaning of Suffering

Quite apart from the pains we inflict upon ourselves through our wrong responses, illegitimate sufferings will necessarily drain our energy to such an extent that we no longer have the strength to shoulder the real crosses that God sends us on our way to salvation.

He will only send us his grace for real, legitimate sufferings if we ask for it. It is futile to expect that God will send us special help to carry pains that are self-manufactured.

There are people whose lives are, humanly speaking, easy and peaceful, and yet they always complain and try to convince us that they truly are martyrs.

But there are people who carry enormous burdens with peaceful cheerfulness and, in spite of crushing crosses, walk through life radiating a light of hope. We might discover after their deaths that they were in constant physical pain and were severely tried in their spiritual life, and yet nothing in their behavior betrayed their secret. We only need read the life of a St. Teresa of Avila, who suffered from ill health throughout her life and whose spiritual trials were of such intensity that only her heroic collaboration with God's grace sustained her. St. Thérèse of Lisieux mentions that most nuns in the Carmel thought that her way was one strewn with roses, and yet she reveals the terrible and horrifying darkness through which she had to struggle for months on end.[21]

It is one of the great Christian mysteries that a person can radiate peace, hope, and even joy while undergoing terrible sufferings. Light is shed on this mystery when we realize that Christianity has given a unique meaning to suffering, and this message is so wonderful that it testifies to the Divinity of its Founder. What other religion invites us to adore and recognize as God a Being who was incarnated in the flesh, lived among men, was condemned to death, suffered agonizing pains, and died crucified in the most atrocious torments? Where Christianity is, we find the God-Man, "who endured the cross, despising the shame".[22] He was indeed the Man of Sorrow, preannounced by Isaiah, "who was despised and rejected by men, . . . acquainted with grief".[23] The Buddha taught the art of escaping from suffering. Muhammad enjoyed fame and recognition. Christ offers us the Cross. It is through the Cross that we have been saved, and it is the Cross that we must embrace if we wish to follow Christ into glory.

Humanly speaking, it is impossible to be attracted by a religion that preaches suffering, renunciation, humility, and death to oneself. And yet the history of Christianity reveals that millions of people, throughout the ages, have abandoned everything to follow Christ to Calvary. This is not masochism but a mystery, and the mystery is love. For "*Deus caritas est*" (God is love)[24], and his love is so infinite that Christ chose suffering and death in order to save sinful humanity from eternal damnation.

Through Christ's sacrifice, the acceptance of suffering has now become a victorious expression of love; St. Paul speaks of it as a Christian privilege: "For it has been granted to you that for the sake of Christ you should not only believe in Him but also suffer for His sake."[25] On this earth, love and suffering cannot be severed; however, it is not suffering that the Christian seeks; it is closeness to the Crucified.

Let us try to show why love and suffering are, on this earth, so deeply intertwined.

Love is linked to suffering. He who starts loving will necessarily start suffering. In spite of the fact that to love and to be loved are the greatest sources of human happiness, to love—on this earth—means also to worry about the loved one. As soon as a person starts loving, he realizes all the perils to which his beloved is exposed and his incapacity to protect him. We all know too well that human life can be snuffed out in a second, that we are constantly exposed to dangers, to sickness, to accidents, to death, and as soon as a person becomes infinitely precious to us, we start trembling for him. I do not know a single mother worthy of this name who does not tremble when she faces the crib of her sick child. I do not know a single lover who does not have to fight against the fear that his beloved might be harmed: an unexplainable weakness, an undiagnosed sickness creates dread and aching; love turns out to be a sweet and yet heavy burden that could easily become unbearable if the Christian could not turn to God and constantly confide his beloved to Christ, he who loves him infinitely more than he himself could. For human love, deep as it is, is only a feeble echo of divine love.

3. The Desire to Share in a Loved One's Suffering

Moreover, it is impossible to love and not to wish to share the trials, sorrows, and sufferings of the loved one. When one loves, one says to the beloved, "From now on, all your joys are my joys; all your sorrows are my sorrows; all your pains are my pains." Gabriel Marcel expresses this strikingly when he writes: "Your death is my death."[26]

On the religious plane, the best way of illuminating this thought is to contemplate the Holy Virgin at the foot of the Cross. All the apostles—except St. John, who came back—had fled. But the Holy Virgin remained, together with the holy women. And she remained because she loved more than the apostles did. For when a woman loves, she fears nothing. All theologians and spiritual writers agree that the Blessed Virgin, while standing at the foot of the Cross, was actually crucified with Christ. Every blow that he received, every nail that pierced his holy flesh, were duplicated in her. This is why she is called Coredemptrix. Her love drove her to share everything with the sacrificial Lamb. Having totally shared his Passion, she now has a unique share in his glory.

On this earth, Christ is found on the Cross, and therefore the Christian embraces the Cross, not because he is attracted by tortures but because his Redeemer is there, agonizing for our sins. Those who love him want to be with him, wherever he happens to be, and therefore they will joyfully shoulder his Cross with him. In eternity, Christ will be found in his glory, and then the theme will be eternal joy. It would be as erroneous to claim proximity to Christ on this earth while pursuing a life of pleasure and enjoyment as it would be to regret that heaven is beatitude and pine over its lack of suffering.

4. Sacrificing Oneself for the Loved One

But the most amazing link between love and suffering is to be found not only in sharing the sorrows and pains of the loved one but also in sacrificing oneself for his sake: "Indeed, there is no greater love than to give one's life for one's friends."[27]

This is precisely what Christ did in accepting to take the form of a slave[28], and the ignominy of the Cross, in order to save us from eternal damnation. This deep and overwhelming truth has been understood by all the saintly souls who, through the centuries of Christian life, have joyfully embraced the Cross and chosen suffering "to complete what is lacking in Christ's afflictions". [29] This is why several great mystics received the stigmata and offer their sufferings united with Christ for the salvation of their brothers. This is why the most severe religious orders (the Carthusians, the Carmelites, the Poor Clares) choose a life of constant suffering and sacrifice and joyfully accept to pay the debt of those who do not love.

When a Christian truly lives the joyful news of the Gospel and is granted the grace to love God and his neighbor in God, he not only is totally liberated from the unbearable weight of illegitimate sufferings but, moreover, becomes capable of carrying heavy crosses in peaceful joy. It is, indeed, this Christian "mystery" that transforms the world's "problem" of suffering. The Christian not only shares the sufferings of the beloved of his soul while united by his own sufferings to Christ on the Cross but, moreover, shares with Christ in his redemptive act. While suffering, the Christian considers his own sufferings a privilege because they are transfigured by love. The Christian is supremely free in that he sees suffering as an expression of his love for Christ on this earth, and this freedom renders him capable to cry over those things that truly call for tears. For being purified by love, and in close union with the Crucified, he is able to perceive what the real sources of sorrow are and echo St. Francis' lament that "the one great sorrow is that Love is so little loved".

NOTES

[1] Pt. II, chap. 4.

[2] *My Prisonenments: Memoirs of Silvio Pellico* (Paris: Baudry European Library, 1837).

[3] *Republic* II, p. 380.

[4] *Etre et Avoir* (Paris: Aubier, 1935).

[5] Gen 1:31.

[6] A Latin translation of a line from Euripides.

[7] Chap. 25.

[8] Dietrich von Hildebrand, *The Heart* (Chicago: Franciscan Herald Press, 1970).

[9] The Rule of St. Benedict, Prologue.

[10] Litany of the Sacred Heart.

[11] Autobiography, Ms. C, pt. II.

[12] *Christian Discourses* (New York: Oxford University Press, 1961), pt. I, chap. 7.

[13] Lk 23:41.

[14] Dietrich von Hildebrand, *Ethics* (Cooperative Freedom) (Chicago: Franciscan Herald Press, 1972), chap. 25.

[15] Cajetan Maria of Bergamo, *Humility of Heart* (Rockford, Ill.: Tan, 1978). Dietrich von Hildebrand, *Transformation in Christ*, chap. VII, "Humility" (Manchester, N.H.: Sophia Institute Press, 1990)

[16] 1 Cor 4:7.

[17] Col 2:7.

[18] *Sickness unto Death* (New York: Doubleday, Anchor Books), pp. 205–6.

[19] Phil 2:7.

[20] Offertory of Holy Mass.

[21] Autobiography, Ms. C, pt. I.

[22] Heb 12:2.

[23] Is 53:3ff.

[24] 1 Jn 4:7, 8, 16.

[25] Phil 1:29.

[26] Roger Troisfontaines, S.J., *De l'Existence l'Etre: La philosophie de Gabriel Marcel*, 2nd ed. (Brussels: Nauwelaerts, S.A., 1968), p. 142.

[27] Jn 15:13.

[28] Phil 2:7.

[29] Col 1:24.